THE
MASTER ANGLER

THE
MASTER
ANGLER

COARSE FISHING SEASON BY SEASON

JOHN BAILEY

CollinsWillow
An Imprint of HarperCollinsPublishers

First published in 1997 by
CollinsWillow
an imprint of HarperCollins*Publishers*
London

1 3 5 7 9 8 6 4 2

A CIP catalogue record for this book
is available from the British Library

ISBN 0 00 218734 5

Photographs by John Bailey and Joy Hicklin-Bailey
with help from their dear friends
Johnny Jensen and Martin Smith

Illustrations by Robert Olsen

Colour reproduction by Colourscan, Singapore

Printed and bound by LEGO SpA, Vicenza, Italy

Contents

Fishing – where a sport becomes an art.

Preface

When I look back on the highs of my life I realize that so many of them have been linked with fishing. I can see that these were moments when a piscatorial puzzle was finally cracked and I took another step up the ladder towards mastering angling.

And yet I know that there will never be an absolute master of the sport, for fishing is simply too deep and too complex for that – hence its eternal and never-waning delight. Let's not cloud the issue, though, because there are, after all, only two basic rules to successful fishing.

The first rule is to locate the fish – a concept so stunningly obvious that all too often it is completely overlooked! It was made absolutely clear to me how important location is when I was seven years of age, three years into my angling career. My tutor was Albert Oldfield, the bailiff on the canal that had been my entire watery world up until then and was indeed for many more years to come. Albert had a bicycle: as simple as that! From the lofty saddle, he would scan the canal for mile after mile until he found fish. Then he would dismount, tackle up, stop selling tickets and start catching. He became nationally famous as a result.

On that momentous day Albert told me my net was dry simply because the fish were 300 yards away. He led me to the spot, showed me the roach priming and asked me why on earth I hadn't used my little legs and my bright eyes to find them for myself! From that day on I vowed never to start fishing unless I was as sure as I possibly could be that I was onto fish in the first place. I've wasted hardly a minute's fishing time ever since.

The second rule, once you've found your fish, is to present a bait that they want to eat and to do so in a way that doesn't alarm them. This all sounds so blissfully simple that you might not believe it could be true. But it is and that's really all there is to fishing!

Of course, it's not always easy to find fish or to put the right bait to them in the right way – and that's where the challenge lies. But at least if we rid our minds of all the rubbish that modern angling's obsession with technique and equipment has built up over the years then we should be able to see the wood for the trees.

In this connection – and I see this as absolutely vital – we must free ourselves from all the modern-day jargon and concentrate on the two simple rules that I've outlined. Only then, I believe, will we both fish better and enjoy our sport more. Fishing will become more immediate, more gripping, and certainly less time will be wasted watching floats that refuse to go under or rod tips that remain obstinately straight! Not only will you have gone a long way towards becoming a Master Angler, but your fishing will be tremendous fun rather than a worry about keeping up with the latest gimmicks.

For as far as I am concerned, you can forget the hype, the endless talk about rigs and baits and tackle. Or at least most of it. Instead, approach fishing with a clear mind and a steady determination, for these qualities are worth a thousand of the latest rigs or the newest bait fads. The Master Angler watches and thinks, keeps mobile and is ready to adapt. He is alert to every mood of the water and every clue that the fish give out. The Master Angler fishes beautifully, cleanly and simply. And above all he enjoys every single minute of it. Now let's look in greater detail at how he does it.

Spring

The really good angler identifies totally with the water before him. In some way, perhaps because of near-dormant instincts passed down from the time when his predecessors were hunters rather than farmers, he can feel the water's rhythms. By that I mean he recognizes the subtle changes that take place in a stillwater or a river from one day to the next, or even during the course of a day. The difference between a very good and an average angler is this awareness of the water. To the first, the water is a friend, giving off positive signals and signs, almost talking to him. However, the angler who never or rarely succeeds sees the water as daunting, a challenge, an element that hides secrets and behaves in an alien, unknowable way.

You only get out of life what you put into it, we say, but it's a platitude that is stunningly true in the case of fishing. If you expect to appear at the water's edge with rods and baits for the first time in a year or more and hope to catch fish of quality then you are probably in for a shock. The anglers around you who are catching fish will be those who have read and absorbed the messages that the water is giving out. The skill is almost a sixth sense, and one that has to be awakened from a deep slumber.

It is in the spring that so much of this learning takes place, and at that time of year the most important equipment that you will take to the water is your eyes and your brain. For the ability to watch and then to form conclusions from what you see is absolutely essential. Of course, there are certain items of

Lily pads are always worth very close observation. All species like the shade given by their leaves and the food that is available on the stems.

equipment that will facilitate all the water watching you will be doing.

Binoculars are an invaluable aid, allowing you to see the most important details that would otherwise be merely a blur. But even more crucial are good Polaroid glasses, as these strip away the watery veil between you and the fish, and seeing fish is the most important first step towards catching them. No serious angler ever goes to the water without his Polaroids; he would feel undressed without them.

Waterproof boots are another essential item. Wellingtons are fine sometimes, but for river work in particular, give me thigh boots or even better, chest-high waders. With chest waders you can enter the water and explore in a hands-on fashion. You will find out in an hour what it takes two days to discover from the bank. Whether it is still or running water, you simply cannot beat getting in there and exploring the fishes' environment for yourself.

A boat – or, even better, a canoe – is another highly efficient way to take exploration one step further. Sometimes a vessel will be available on the water that you are investigating and if it's safe and you are confident about using it, then do so – you will be amazed at what you find out. My own canoe, a Kiwi, is light, broad-beamed and supremely stable, so that I can take it into the shallowest water and hardly make a ripple. I've crept up on all types of freshwater fish and they seem to think I'm no more than a passing swan or a drifting clump of weed. Approaching a fish so close, seeing it so intimately in its natural environment, is pretty near as good as actually catching it.

Whether you're going out from the bank

A canoe is the perfect tool for exploring all waters but most especially canals. This is best done in the close season, when they tend to be at their quietest. Look out for all features that could harbour fish later on throughout the season and also, make a note of any shoals that you come across, for it could be that they will stay in the area for at least part of the summer.

in waders or by boat, do be careful. Never take risks, and never do anything that you are not happy with. Keep your eye constantly on the weather and beware of any mounting wind or storm – remember that in the springtime a squall can blow up from nowhere. Make sure that your thigh boots or waders have reliable soles and wear buoyancy aids at all times. If you plan to go out from the bank, then do so only if you have a friend on the bank with both the knowledge and the means to help you. Do not venture out alone. And remember that a rope is a simple investment that can save a life.

In the spring, choose your exploring days carefully: going out when the weather is calm, bright and settled will increase your efficiency tenfold. By contrast, if you are not enjoying yourself because of the weather, you may well decide to go home early, with the job half done. Water clarity is an important allied consideration. On many lakes the bottom lifts off in the spring as the water warms and the dead weed from the previous year comes to the surface. If the water is at all choppy then this weed breaks up, creates a cloud and prevents accurate observation. Also, if the weather has been very hot for some time there may well be an equally irritating algal bloom which can turn the water into pea soup overnight.

Ideally, arrive at your chosen water as dawn breaks and stay there until last light, learning everything about it through all the daylight hours. What you see at dawn can be fascinating, but what is revealed at dusk can

be essential. Also, throughout the day, when the light is at its greatest, you will be able to do the bulk of your investigative work.

It's vital to remember exactly what you've learnt and I always take with me a large A4 notepad. Or you can use a plain artist's sketch book and put the time, date and place on each page, along with your observations. Draw maps of the whole water and then larger-scale

maps of areas that you have looked at closely. Mark in all depth contours, the composition of the bottom, emerging weedbeds, fallen trees, pieces of masonry, sightings of fish – in fact, anything that could make that little bit of difference once you begin to fish in earnest.

I keep my notepads for ever, safely stacked away in the study, and they make fascinating reading. No water ever remains the same: all are dynamic, in a state of flux, changing from one year to the next. On rivers, especially large ones, the changes can be very marked, for each winter's floods can alter a swim almost beyond recognition. It's fascinating to compare a favourite spot from one season to the next with the help of your notebook. In fact, this exercise can prove invaluable, for often it reveals the secret movements of fish.

Life at the Waterside

Spring is the most dynamic of all the seasons for the creatures that live on, in or around the water. Rivers and stillwaters explode into life after the deadness of the winter: you can feel the vitality, see nature vibrant, bursting to make up for those months of cold and inaction. Everything meshes, wheels turn within wheels, and by being alert to it, absorbing it all, you will gain valuable insights into the waters you want to know better.

Let's look at a few examples. Posses of herons gather on the shallows of rivers dawn after dawn, secure in the knowledge that barbel and chub, dace and roach will be there to spawn, presenting an easy meal. There these predators will stand as the sun rises, pillars of grey emerging from the mists. Often they simply slash at fish far too large for them to eat but they will also find small chub, dace, elvers and lampreys all moving past, easy prey for that scything beak. They find larger eels

Herons gather around the shallows at dawn looking for all sorts of pickings. Of course, it's not just spawning fish that they're after but all manner of things that might interest the angler – big dace perhaps, or bullhead, loach and gudgeon that would do nicely for baits for barbel and chub at this time of year.

too, fish of nearly 1lb and quite easily swallowed, eels that have been attracted by the spawning barbel and are eager to eat their eggs. Clearly, for all their predations, the herons are doing the barbel a service and without them the eels would go unpunished and their number would swell immeasurably.

This is the time of year when grebes will be hunting avidly: they have a nest of young hidden in the reeds who need to feed constantly. One grebe or another will be at work all the time, scanning the lake, following the fleeing roach shoals. The serious angler will watch all this, make notes on what is going on and understand that the pike and perch will be acting in much the same way as the grebes, fish and birds – both aware of exactly when and where the great shoals of prey are moving.

At this time of year the riverbanks are quieter and now is your best chance of all to see that most beautiful of aquatic animals, the otter. Sightings are rare but the evidence is that otters are returning to many parts of the country, although you'll

Grebes have to hunt very hard in the spring, particularly if they often have a family to feed. If you watch them carefully you begin to get some idea of where the roach shoals are holing up.

Success for the grebe and its family.

A nesting coot building in the branches of a waterlogged tree. Such places should be taken note of because they are the type of area that carp flock to later in the year when the temperatures begin to drop.

need to be quite and it's almost essential to be at the water long before sunrise. Choose a high area that gives a fine overall view of the river above and below. Then sit in perfect silence listening, hoping to hear that keen, piercing whistle that a hunting and travelling otter makes. Even through binoculars, at first you may see only a small black dot bobbing ball-like on the surface of the river. But remain still and well hidden and the animal will come closer, possibly passing within a few yards of you. Who knows, you may see it hunt and come up with a 2lb chub or eel writhing in its jaws. Then it will be gone, off downstream to some holt in the bank where it will spend the daylight hours.

You may ask what the use of all this is

to the man intent on catching fish alone. Perhaps there are no clear lessons to be learned, but if this is your attitude then, sadly, to you the waterside will remain one-dimensional, uninspiring; it will never reach out and embrace you, or yield up its secrets. By contrast, the angler who learns to see and puts his insight to practical use will benefit from every waterside observation he makes.

Tarka out and about! To see an otter on a river is a very good sign indeed because they need a high density of fish if they are to remain present in the area. If there are few fish then you won't see otters – they will simply have moved on to more fertile waters.

Now is the time to spot the toads swarming from the ditches in their thousands.

Spawning

Pike especially, and perch to some extent, spawn very early in the year, but most of our freshwater species do so later, many of them in May, when the water begins to really warm up for the first time. In stillwater, roach and bream are among the first to spawn, with tench and carp following later – generally from June onwards, depending on the weather.

In the rivers, chub and barbel head for gravels during May, then wait in the area for the sun to get to work. Chub generally spawn first, with barbel beginning to thrash the surface in the first week or two in June. Nearly all the population of a stretch will decamp to shallow gravel runs, and once you've located these fish, the sight is awesome.

In my experience, barbel too spawn most easily around about sunrise. Of course, they will be busy at other times but at that point when the water is like molten gold they seem to reach a crescendo. Chub seem more obliging and will certainly spawn in bright daylight, though once again the early morning seems to be favoured.

Bream are probably the most dramatic spawners of the stillwater species, again moving into great shoals that may well embrace the entire population of the lake. Spawning tends to take place from early morning to around lunchtime and then interest starts to wane. A similar period, from early morning until about ten or eleven o'clock, sees most of the carp spawning activity. Very often you can hear them spawning when you are as far as

Spawning has begun and a number of fish are milling around closer and closer, in many cases only inches from the bank.

200-300 yards from the water. The sound is volcanic. Indeed, so obsessed with spawning do carp become that very frequently they will lever themselves out of the water, marooning themselves on the bank. In fact, it's a piece of good luck for the fish if a caring angler is there witnessing these events, since he or she can save the life of an otherwise stranded fish.

But what can the angler learn by witnessing this primeval event? For one thing a great deal of nonsense is talked about fish populations by those who simply don't know. You will hear gossip to the effect that a lake is either stuffed with, say, bream or pretty well barren of them. But if you watch the water at spawning time then you will gain at first hand a

Carp spawning wildly – you can get close enough to touch them in circumstances like this so it's an ideal opportunity to investigate what the fish stocks of the water are.

pretty accurate idea of its fish stocks. That knowledge may well come in useful later.

Just as much nonsense is talked about the size of particular fish. We all know exactly the type of thing: bream in here to 10lb, carp in there to well over 30lb and so on. However, if at spawning time the largest bream you see is 5lb, then why are all these shadowy monsters of double figures keeping themselves hidden?

All knowledge about fish is good, and by watching them like this you will begin to appreciate much more the dignity and the grace of your quarry. In addition, seeing the most private aspects of their lives puts you in tune with them, so that you will henceforth be more careful to guard them against those that would harm them. If we accept that to become a Master Angler is to form a powerful bond with fish and the water they inhabit, then springtime observations like these can only be for the good of all concerned.

Spring Rivers

Bridges

There's an angling book from the 1930s which has a chapter called 'Leaners'. Every bridge over every river, it says, has its occupational leaner, a man who spends most of his time, at least until the pub opens, with his hands on the bridge parapet, his eyes glued to the water below. A man like this, believed the author, can be of great help to the angler, telling him exactly what's passed up-river during the last week or so, or simply what fish are in the vicinity.

What that writer observed is still true. There is indeed something about bridges which seems to be a magnet for fishermen as well as fish. It is partly a question of currents. Current speed and direction are both vital to fish and dictate strongly where and when they will lie up. Clearly, a bridge squeezes the river, like a lady pouring herself into a corset, and this produces all sorts of effects on the current, changes that we as land-dwelling animals can never appreciate. But fish can and do sense them. A good example is when the current speeds up a little bit or takes a

Left: A view from a bridge. Springtime is the perfect opportunity to watch fish carefully from bridges, especially when there is sand or gravel beneath that might attract them in to spawn. Make it a rule to visit bridges regularly, especially in the morning, when the fish are likely to be still on the shallows before returning to deeper water as the light grows.

Below: In this detailed picture of a bridge you can see for yourself how the buttresses narrow the span of the river, forcing the water into a corset. This makes for a deep, steady pool, prized by roach throughout the year. The cattle coming down to drink only add to the attraction of the place by muddying the water and releasing food.

The lower parts of bridges often provide a good base to fish from. Remember, the closer you can get to the fish, the better your bait control is bound to be – providing of course you don't scare the fish off with a clumsy approach. Here the bridge pillars provide excellent screening.

slightly new direction that proves irresistible to the fish.

Inevitably the current does speed up around bridges, but also it often scours the bottom, clearing away silt, exposing gravel and stones. This is a vital factor, because a clear, shining bottom produces more food. Look under any stone near a bridge and it is likely to be crawling with life.

There will also be a bridge pool, a downstream area that is deeper than the rest of the surrounding river and has, over the decades, been gouged out by the currents. Deep water is always irresistible to fish at certain times of the year but I'm sure that their liking for bridge pools also has something to do with the shade afforded by the structure of the bridge itself. For much of the day the brick or metal columns keep direct sunlight off the water and cast an air of gloom immediately below them. Fish are extremely sensitive to light and even a

This is an old toll-bridge, now disused and replaced by a new structure downstream. The interesting thing is that the old bridge seems to offer far more attractions to the fish — roach, chub and barbel in particular flock there while ignoring the new one altogether. The lure of the place has a lot to do with the amount of rubble and old masonry on the bed of the river.

narrow bridge can prove a real blessing in offering vital shade.

Now let's look back over the history of an imaginary but typical bridge. What about all that masonry that has fallen off it during its lifetime? The more rubble that has fallen in, the more homes there are for tiny aquatic creatures, destined frequently to become food for the fishes. You can see what's happened over the decades or even centuries: the bridge has been bashed by carts and cars and stones

or bricks have tumbled into the river below. More homes for grubs and beetles and bullheads, more shelter from the winter floods for barbel and chub. And what about those trolleys and prams or old bicycles thrown in at the dead of night? Think how they too gather the weed and dead branches washed down over the winter and provide further forms of shelter.

Spring is certainly the time to be out on bridges, watching. It's during May that many roach and chub migrate up-river, looking for spawning sites on clear gravel – often near the bridge. It's frequently very difficult to know exactly what a stretch of river holds and you need to get every bit of help you can. A bridge gives the most perfect vantage-point for looking down deep into the water, seeing exactly what the stocks of the river are.

From a bridge, through April and May, I've seen roach, chub and barbel that have made me gasp and that have revealed far more about the stretch in question than I'd ever guessed in weeks of walking the banks. In fact one or two of my best-ever fish came directly as a result of observation that I carried out from a bridge for a great part of the close season. You can be sure that every minute spent 'leaning' is well spent, for every minute could throw up a clue that could change your angling fortunes.

Hunting under the Stones

If you fish in mainland Europe you'll often see anglers hunting under the boulders around bridges or along the banks of rivers. They'll have buckets with them in which to place any enticing food items that they unearth. Continental anglers are much more aware of the natural foodstuffs that our river species eat and are far more willing to use them as bait. In Britain, we are much more concerned with persuading the fish to take what we have to offer them – maggots, casters, hempseed and the like.

Last season I was able to entice barbel with lobworms, brandlings and, from under the stones, caddis larvae, bullheads, stonefly nymphs, snails and, truthfully, three tiny black leeches on a size 12 hook.

The great beauty of this type of bait is that it is inexpensive and the fish are also immediately turned on – after all, this is the food they are used to eating and are actively on the lookout for.

The spring is the perfect opportunity to investigate the food sources of your local river and become expert at uncovering tempting untried morsels.

The twaite shad, unfamiliar to many anglers, is one of our most exciting fishes. In May and June it swims up the Wye and Severn and Ireland's Shannon towards its spawning beds.

Spring Stillwaters

— Lakes in Springtime —

Most lakes have weed, and fish like weed for a variety of reasons – that much is certain. But I'm not one of those anglers who put much store by 'reading' weed, its density and the types fish favour, hoping to predict a pattern in their behaviour for the coming season.

In the spring it's obviously important to establish where the weedbeds are and how they are growing, for this will give you some indication of where fish are holed up and where they might be travelling to and from. At this time of year you might also be thinking about cutting back some weed,

A female fish has been lifted right up by accompanying males and is about to be thrown out of the water. By acting quickly you can save a fish's life at this time of year if this happens.

especially if it looks like a particularly promising area might be almost impossible to fish because of weed growth. However, considering just how fast weed can grow, it's often best to wait until just before a fishing session to do any actual cutting.

No, when it comes to investigating springtime lakes, rather than spend much thought or effort on weed I believe the Master Angler should look specifically at bottom make-up. In any average lake there will almost certainly be pockets here and there where fish feed hard and other regions that they simply travel through. In my experience, the key is a clean, hard bottom, of sand, gravel or even chalk. Almost none of the species like feeding over thick silt or slimy mud, and tend to avoid it as much as possible. Therefore so should you when picking swims or places to pre-bait.

Left: A large dead bream found floating a few days after spawning. This is a natural part of aquatic life, so do not jump to the conclusion that the cause is pollution or an outbreak of disease.

Left: A large dead bream found floating a few days after spawning. This is a natural part of aquatic life, so do not jump to the conclusion that the cause is pollution or an outbreak of disease.

Right: Late spring and already the stillwater is beginning to explode with life and colour.

Areas of the bed remain clean of rubbish for several reasons: very often debris accumulates in dips or troughs in the bed, pushed there by the wind or sub-surface currents. The point where springs enter the lake often remain clear of all rubbish too, as do those places where a wave action hits a steeply descending bank. Whatever the reason, what you are looking for is a good clean lake bed and once you have found such areas you can be fairly sure you have found places where fish will feed. Usually these places grow bigger because the more often fish feed on them, the more silt and weed are kept at bay.

You can spot these areas in various ways: either from the bank with Polaroids and binoculars or by climbing trees and scanning the bottom carefully. Alternatively, you can paddle around in a boat or canoe and look closely at the water that way. The other option – provided you are *totally* sure that the bed is not soft or otherwise dangerous and that you will *never* be out of your depth – is to wade in thigh-boots or chest waders, equipped with a good hard landing-net pole, prodding around for the sort of features I've already mentioned above.

It will be clear by now that I see a clean bottom as the place on which to concentrate your energies. The question that now arises is the vexed issue of pre-baiting. Is it worthwhile? How often should you do it? How much bait should you introduce? Ideally, you would pre-bait quite heavily with a bait you know the fish like, in an area where they are wont to feed. The problem is that very often you won't be able to afford the time or the money to get to the lake often enough to pre-bait regularly. But if you can, make the best of it, for there is absolutely no doubt that the more bait you put in on a regular basis the more often fish will go there to look out for it, and the more likely you are to catch them.

Rest assured, though, that even if you can only get to the water a few times before fishing begins and put in moderate amounts of bait, this will still pay dividends. And, if you are lucky, you might see the fish feed on the food that you are introducing, which cannot fail to boost your confidence about the sessions in prospect.

If you're a carp angler you will almost certainly want to start introducing the new boiled baits that you have been working on throughout the winter. It's very unlikely that you'll want to go to the water cold, without having put in any new bait at all. There are various considerations here: for example, how many fish per acre do you reckon the lake holds? Will you be putting a lot of baits in only for ducks to dive and eat them once you have gone? Sit down and plan your strategy carefully rather than just take 200 baits to a water and hurl them out willy-nilly. That is

simply to mistake quantity for quality. Whatever bait you're introducing, it's best to put it out at last light so that water birds have less chance of seeing it in the darkness or, for that matter, seeing you throwing it in. Alternatively, put it out early in the day and then stay as long as possible just to ease your mind that it is staying in the water rather than ending up in some bird's gullet! Bear in mind that whether you are using boilies, sweetcorn, bread or anything else, if ducks are a problem then if you pre-bait a little more closely in you will be more able to scare them away by waving your arms. Another tip is to drive birds away by pointing a closed umbrella at them and then opening it and shutting it quickly and violently. They hate the sight and are terrified of the sound, and usually will just vanish.

Below: In springtime, when waters are generally less busy, fish of all species come closer to the margins. It's quite common to see tench, for example, browsing just a yard or so from the bank.

Right: One of the first really hot days of the year and the lake glows under the sunshine. Look at that drop-off just a rod length out and imagine how tench will love to follow it, browsing on the shelf and also moving into the very shallow water when there is a chance of food.

You will find that in springtime tench are often very visible, moving up and down certain areas of the bank – especially through the mid and late morning. They tend to drift away sometime after midday on most lakes that I know, so it pays to get to the waterside early. What you will almost certainly find is that specific fish stick to certain margins of the lake with very little overlap.

Another thing you'll discover is that here and there the bigger fish tend to keep to themselves, so very careful observation really does pay off when it comes to the actual sessions. Almost certainly you will find that certain areas of the lake hold predominantly small fish whereas other marginal areas seem to attract the big ones. These different sizes

A lovely stillwater full of excitement and interest for the springtime observer. Here there are bays where fish may be spawning and all sorts of areas in which to study fish feeding and travelling.

of fish tend to build up their territories and stick to them throughout the summer, so that identifying these areas really puts you in the driving seat.

It's much the same with bream, for shoals do seem to stick to their own patrol routes around the lake. The more clues you have from watching with binoculars the more likely you will be to pre-bait the right patrol route and catch the sort of fish that you are after. With both tench and bream it's surprising how quickly you can build up a picture of the movements of groups, and even of individuals.

There is nothing more demoralizing than fishing a large lake and not feeling sure if your bait is near fish at all. However, when you know that you have placed it on a nice

hard bottom where fish are likely to feed, and that particular spot is within the patrol route of tench or bream, then your confidence will rocket. So will your catches.

There are all sorts of other clues to be gleaned at this time of year when waters are likely to be a little bit quieter. For example, if there are any landing-stages around the lake approach these very carefully indeed. The reason is that very often at this time of year perch clean or scratch their bodies against any piece of timber set into the lake bed. You can often get very close to them and when you do you may well get a surprise. Often I have found big perch in a lake where I was not even sure the species existed.

Look out, too, for spawning carp. Spawning often begins in early June, especially when it is very hot. Not only is it exciting to watch spawning carp but it also gives you a reliable impression of how many fish there are in the lake and what the maximum size might be. During spawning,

Detecting Crucian Carp

Carp, tench and bream we see often enough in the springtime. But what about the fish that we see less frequently? What about the elusive crucian carp, for example? Delightful to look at and fascinating in their habits, crucians are a real challenge for any angler. And spring, especially late spring, is the perfect time to look out for signs of them in lakes.

You might well see crucians spawning – small clumps of fish shedding their eggs vigorously on hard weed around the margins. Or, if you're very lucky, you might see them browsing just beneath the surface, or resting around lily pads – it's quite wrong to think these fish are exclusively bottom feeders. And be careful about identification, for a large crucian can easily be mistaken in the water for a small common carp. Then again, you might see a crucian roll in its typical splashy way. At first you'll be taken by surprise but if you really focus and see another one or two come out you might well be able to make your mind up.

Most crucian carp remain uncaught for the simple reason that anglers have no idea that they are present in the water. If you know they are there, if you've seen them and if you know something of their patrol routes, then you are at least halfway to putting them on the bank. Try some light groundbaiting with very finely mashed bread laced with casters, hempseed or minced-up sweetcorn. Crucians love small, sloppy, smelly foodstuffs and you could soon have these beautiful little fish really fizzing over the bait.

This beautifully conditioned crucian carp fell to a large piece of slowly sinking flake on the edge of a weedbed.

carp seem absolutely without fear of man and you can get within touching distance of them when they are thrashing around in marginal reed and rushes. Once again this will give you not only a deeper knowledge of the lake stocks but also a growing confidence that you know your water intimately.

The effect of all this quiet observation is to build up a picture of the water that is constantly in your mind's eye. Even if you are not at the lake you will be thinking about it, confident of where the carp, bream or tench will be moving or feeding.

The more your mind works like this the more ideas spring into it and the greater your confidence grows. I said in the introduction to this book that the two fundamental rules to mastering angling are locating fish and then presenting a desirable bait in a natural way. I could have added a third rule, although because it's a state of mind rather than a course of action it's less easy to describe. That indispensable quality is confidence. Quite why confidence is so important, no angler has ever fully explained, yet it remains a fact agreed on by every successful fisherman.

A Picture in Depth

When it comes to checking the depth of a water we all have our own favourite method, which may or may not be one of several tried-and-tested techniques. Probably the most popular plumbing method is to attach a medium-sized pike float, bottom end only, to the line by means of a link and swivel, and at the end of that line tie on a 2–3oz bomb.

Before you begin plumbing, draw a rough diagram of the water so that you can compile a quick-reference chart of depths. Now cast out in the various lines that you think you will be fishing later, wait until your line has sunk and then wind in until the float is tight against the lead. The bomb will make casting easy, but don't cast too far or you will be plumbing far beyond where you can place a bait. The set-up will now be very tight, with the lead, float and most of the line on the bed of the water. Now simply open your bale arm and pay out line, allowing your float to rise. Perhaps put a marker on your rod about a foot up from the reel so that you know exactly how much line you have

paid out by the time the float arrives on the surface.

Once you see the float, simply multiply by one foot the number of times you released the line to the marker and you will have a precise depth. Record the depth information on the diagram and then wind in two to three yards of line until everything is tight again.

Now repeat the process, but this time casting four or five yards to both left and right of the original line and recording the depths on your chart. You'll be amazed how quickly you build up a detailed picture of the bottom of the water – an essential asset for those long sessions when accurate groundbaiting and casting are of prime importance in boosting your chances.

A final tip: make sure that the pike float is attached to the line by a link swivel. If instead you put the line straight through the plastic eye the strain of constant casting and winding will soon weaken it or even break it off. Pike floats are not cheap, so treat them carefully.

The Monster of the Bay

For many years now it has been accepted that pike in the large, clear, colder waters flock to bays to spawn during April and May. For centuries this has been the time that monster pike have been seen or landed in both Scotland and Ireland. Modern anglers have been aware of this phenomenon too, particularly since the 1960s, when Loch Lomond emerged as a premier pike water. The bays became famous, huge fish were caught and for many pike anglers the spring pilgrimage is now a vital part of their year.

Bays are always a magnet for pike on huge waters when the spawning season approaches. Once the water warms, the big females begin to move into the shallow water slightly after the smaller males have arrived. This pattern repeats itself on large waters throughout Ireland, Scotland, the Lake District and northern Europe.

However, let's travel to the saline bays on the southern Swedish coastline, to look at a rather special fish and the message delivered by its capture.

Coastal pike – like perch – are capable of living in water with a degree of salinity and certainly, in the salt-poor waters of the Baltic around Sweden's coastline, they thrive. There the sea pike grow enormous, feeding on codling, burbot and herring. For most of the year the really big pike lie around islands two to three miles offshore, intercepting shoals of sea fish as they follow the currents. But in April, when the water temperatures rise, the hormones begin to stir and these huge pike begin their annual journey into the bays that lie between the coast and the inland forests.

These bays are like those in Scotland and Ireland: shallow, clear and quick to warm. In Sweden, once the winds turn from the south and the days pull out, then the pike begin to move in in droves. They can still be caught in

the sea, at the mouth of these bays, but for the very biggest fish it is wise to take a boat in, close to the forest line, and even stalk individuals. This is exactly how Johnny Jensen landed his monster and there is a message here for all pike anglers.

We knew that the pike were beginning their migration and coming thick and fast: on the Tuesday we had taken a 29lb fish and on the Wednesday several of 15–25lb. It was on that day that Johnny saw his monster. The pike had followed his lure once or twice, showing some sort of interest in it before veering off, leaving a big bow-wave and a cloud of silt the size of a sitting-room.

On the Thursday Johnny just poled around the water, hour after hour, looking for the huge female through Polaroid glasses. Once or twice he saw her in the late

An absolutely magnificent fish of just under 30lb. This great pike pursued the lure – a double-jointed green one – right to the boat before making any decision. The angler was then alert enough to see the fish and move his lure round in a tight, frenetic figure-of-eight movement right under the boat itself. The impressive result we can all see. It really does pay to wear Polaroids when fishing from a boat with a lure because these allow you to see what is going on underneath the water.

afternoon, when clarity was at its height. The fish was not really resting, but moving, agitated, probably looking for partners.

And so it was on Friday: the morning proved fruitless apart from one sighting of the fish, close to a reedbed and travelling at speed. We all stopped for lunch, Johnny quiet, his thoughts firmly on that bay. And it was there he returned in the mid-afternoon, once more drifting on the breeze, looking for that fish.

But it was she who found him! Out of nowhere the giant loomed, swimming abreast of his plug – not, as you would expect, behind it. No, for 10 yards the pike swam eyeball to eyeball with the plug, no more than a foot to its right and matching its speed perfectly. Johnny was in absolute confusion. It took a lot of nerve to carry on

Another good pike caught through observation. This fish again followed a lure that kept veering away, and only fell to a livebait put in its path.

rowing at the same steady pace with the fish just eight yards or so from the boat.

Then, after thirty seconds, the pike simply moved her head and the plug was gone. Johnny blinked but there was still no plug. He picked up the rod, struck and the water exploded. Hook one of these big pike at this time of the year in a shallow, clear bay and you'll need the strongest, most reliable pike tackle that you can lay your hands on. For twenty minutes the fish surged almost uncontrollably in the water before, finally, it was brought to the net.

There was never a pike like that one. I remember thinking that its eyeballs were like

It's doubtful whether you'll ever see a bigger pike than this on the bank – nearly 47lb. What you can't get from the photograph is its immense width and depth – these are the dimensions that really separate monster pike from ordinary fish.

Return the fish with the greatest possible care. Whatever fish you are putting back, hold it until it is upright and the fins are working strongly. Never release a fish if you think it could go belly up a few yards out in deep water where you will be unable to help it.

a sheep's and that its skin was as grooved and gnarled as an ancient oak. I also remember the width across the shoulders and then lifting the fish from the water; the belly just went on and on and on. My own estimations of its size just kept increasing.

Sadly, we did not have scales man enough for the job of weighing that historic fish. All we can say is that it was approaching 47lb – perhaps a few ounces below. Johnny had been on the trail of that pike for days, he had forsaken all the others – good fish too – that were present in that bay and the inlets surrounding it. He had his sights on that one fish and he was content to wait until the moment it should decide to feed. His approach was perfect. He moved his boat around the water like a shadow, his awareness was constant and once he crossed paths with that huge specimen his nerve never faltered. Rarely can such a monster of a fish have been so richly deserved.

My expeditions to Sweden have brought home several vital lessons, many applicable to the UK pike scene. First and foremost, you cannot take these big, careful fish for fools, even though the spawning urge is on them. Very careful boat practice must be observed, for trolling over water less than 12ft deep can be suicidal.

Secondly, lure fishing can be a good taking method but often it succeeds very well in annoying pike, sparking them into taking a livebait or deadbait. When lure fishing, always wear Polaroids so that you can watch for follows, and have a natural bait at the ready for the pike that refuses to commit itself to plastic.

Fish especially hard at dawn, as many fish move from deeper to shallower water under the cover of night and first light can see them there for the catching. This is especially so if a warm wind – say from the south or the west – is pushing into the bay itself.

Lastly, if the bay is shallow and clear enough it often pays to drift with the wind, simply looking for big fish. Without oars or engine, you won't disturb pike unless you go right over them, so that this tactic is highly effective for pinpoint location.

Pike Stalking

While you're wandering along the banks of large rivers in April, May and early June, It always pays to keep an eye out for pike. Very often at that time of year they drift into the slacks and shallows to pick up a dead or dying shad, ambush some spawning roach or simply to rest from the main force of the current.

The purpose of this exercise is not so much to locate small or medium pike as to form some idea of the big pike that could be present in that particular water. It's very easy to concentrate on chub, roach or barbel and ignore pike stocks altogether.

However, on many rivers very large pike exist and their presence is barely suspected at all. This is the time of the year when their presence can be noted most easily, although you may have to look very hard into the water to see even a big fish, so perfect is the species' camouflage. Once you've found pike, you should also note the areas of river that they inhabit.

So, if you spot some really tempting fish as you rove the banks, be sure to come back in the late summer and try those places with a suitable spinner, deadbait or other offering.

Summer

On stillwaters and rivers alike, summer is a time of plenty – the really golden period when weed growth is at its most prolific and food stocks abound. This is just as well for all our species of fish, which are recovering after the exertions of spawning and frequently indulge in heavy feeding which needs to be easy and stress-free.

This abundance can bring problems. For example, in lakes where certain weeds can grow a foot in twenty-four hours, even extensive raking is not enough to ensure good sport. And then natural food, when plentiful enough, can prove a major headache for anglers, as most fish species become preoccupied with food items that are far too small or individual to copy with bait. Daphnia is the perfect example of this, and there are times when bream and tench will follow columns of these water-fleas around a stillwater, sipping them in, oblivious to anything larger than a pinhead.

Nor does extreme heat help the angler. There are unrelenting, albeit brief, periods during most British summers when the water seems like a furnace and the fish languish, not once making a mouth at anything. Lack of rain goes with these periods too; lakes become stale and the levels drop. Rivers suffer even more and normally lively flows dwindle to a canal-like pace. In both cases, fish respond accordingly and you can almost see their fins droop!

Bright sunlight can also work to the angler's detriment, burning fish off the shallows and forcing them into dense weed or impenetrable snags. Summer is also the time of year when most waters are at their busiest – perhaps with tourists eager for a break from the beach or anglers understandably keen to get to the bankside after the privations of the close season.

But summer has its up side too: clear water, bright light and pleasing warmth all encourage expansive fishing. No longer do you have to sit huddled under an umbrella, swathed in waterproof and thermal clothing. Now you can wander the banks, and experiment with new methods and baits. Best of all, in the clear summer water and under a high, unclouded sun, you can watch the fishes' reaction to your innovations, and form some useful conclusions.

For me the summer offers the peak of the year's fishing. It is the time when I want to be on the water as much as possible, when I feel in total harmony and at peace with it. Twenty-four hours a day is not too long to be at the water when the nights are mild and the days are warm and you can sleep for a short while on the grass under a tree and wake up without a sniffle. The fish may not be at their biggest, nor at their easiest to catch, but who cares if you can pursue them in interesting and exciting ways?

A few points about summer fishing are worth mentioning.

- Don't stay out all day without the right strength of sun blocker on your nose and arms and legs (if uncovered) and do wear a hat of one form or another.
- Take plenty of water and keep it cool in the margins or in shade.
- Mosquito repellent can be very useful on

Canals can be long, straight and featureless, and that's why it's so important to make every bit of use of any clues to location. Reedbeds, for example, are an absolute magnet to all fish species.

many waters, especially at dawn and dusk, and on some, if you're going to maintain your sanity you will need a special hat to protect you from midges.

- Unless you are absolutely convinced of dry weather, it's a good idea to take with you a light waterproof jacket, as a summer shower can leave you feeling cold for a long time afterwards.
- If you are staying out all night, note that summer temperatures can drop dramatically, and prepare yourself as if for a winter daytime session.

This may all sound like common sense, but, apart from the safety aspect, there's a good reason for stressing it. You can't master angling unless your mind is really on the job, so if you are distracted by problems like insects and feeling wet and cold, or you become sunburnt, you won't be fishing to the best of your ability at all.

Summer Rivers

The Rock

Rocks always attract barbel and the bigger the rocks the more barbel there are likely to be in the area. Trying to read the mind of fish is a risky business, but I think you can probably see the reasons for this species' fascination with rocks. For a start, they adore overhangs, and a large rock or series of rocks offers plenty of these. Furthermore, barbel enjoy areas where there is a variation of currents and obviously a rock breaks up the major flow of the river and diverts it in many ways attractive to them.

Finally, barbel are always thinking about food stocks and there is no doubt that an expanse of rock strongly attracts all sorts of larvae and grubs. There's probably more that barbel are drawn to, but at least we have some reliable clues to their preferences.

The main problem is that rocky areas are not easy to fish and that's certainly what I found on one particular swim on a large river. Now, I had seen big barbel flash around the enormous rock from the hillside above the river. It was awe-inspiring to gaze down 100ft or more and see those splendid fish turn over lazily, flashing gleams of gold. But how could I catch them?

I made my way back to the south bank of the river, cut through the undergrowth and finally reached the shingle banks from where, I decided, I would launch my attack. The question was: what sort of attack? The rock was about the size of a small car and barbel were turning all around it but most noticeably in its lee, among an extensive carpet of smaller jagged stones. That was the obvious place to put a bait and the conventional response would have been to sling a feeder over and let it settle in the slacker water around the main rock, where the barbel were feeding.

But there were a number of problems with this, most noticeably my fear of constant snagging in such a treacherous area. Also, the strength of the main currents would be continually creating bows in the line, so that sensitivity to bites would be seriously reduced. In addition, the water behind the rock was only about 3ft deep, and I suspected that the splash of a feeder could hardly fail to upset the barbel.

Nevertheless, the solution looked quite simple: in front of the sunken rock stood a second large rock, this one with its top exposed. It would be quite possible to wade the river to this first rock and then trot a bait

Above: This rock is huge and bound to attract barbel. In fact if you look closely you can see one flashing at the far side, just downstream – a typical holding area for fish.

Right: I'm fascinated, watching the fish. But just look at that rock close to me with its head out of the water. The water round it is no more than 4½ft deep and the currents are slow, so it will be quite safe for me to wade over to this unusual fishing platform.

Above: Don't hesitate to use any fishing station, no matter how small, if there is room for you to sit with a net and a bait can. Accessories, such as floats, shot and hooks, can easily be carried in a pocket. However, don't take risks in reaching the spot.

Left: A good deep net is imperative for fishing situations like this. Never be seduced into buying the shallow, pan-type nets that matchmen like. If you are really exploring a water there may be times when you've got to carry a fish through difficult terrain so you want to make sure that it's safe and will not escape if you take a spill.

Right: Posing with the fish for just an instant – half in and half out of the water. In this way, if it wriggled I could direct it into the water rather than onto gravel.

around the sunken boulder and present it with absolute efficiency, naturalness and no hint of disturbance.

I returned later in the afternoon, when the sun was more fully on the water. With shorts on, I waded out and began to bait the area heavily with sweetcorn. Soon the barbel were flashing merrily, clearly taking the grains. I sat there for half an hour, feeding in more and more bait, and at the end of that time smaller fish were actually coming off the bottom to take the falling corn in mid-water or even just below the surface – a fascinating sight.

There were one or two very fine barbel in the swim, keeping slightly deeper, rarely coming off the bottom at all, and it was fish like these that I had my eye on. Obviously the bait would have to be trotted slow and deep to interest these fish. But that wouldn't

be a problem as I was sitting only seven or eight yards from them and could see quite clearly their reaction to everything going on around them.

Tackle was straightforward: a 12ft 1¼lb test-curve rod, 6lb b.s. line straight through to a size 10 hook and two grains of sweetcorn. The float was a big crystal stick, with the shot evenly spaced down the line apart from a slight cluster 6in from the hook just to get the bait down quickly and keep it in that bottom area.

I had decided on corn because barbel cannot resist it unless they have succumbed to it already and taken a real hammering. Worms would have been as instant in their effect but corn, I knew, would really get the fish into a feeding frenzy and even break them up a little bit so that I could then

concentrate on one or two of the best.

The sun was fairly high now and illuminated the whole scene right beneath my dangling feet. Often barbel would come close to my own rock, attracted by grains of corn that had fallen in from my bucket. As yet, I hadn't made a cast – I was just looking for the size of fish that I was after. And then, I saw it – very tight to the sunken boulder itself, working backwards and forwards across the current, intercepting corn that had gone down deep.

I set the float about 1ft over-depth and swung it some three yards upstream of the rock, holding it back carefully. The bait trundled towards the barbel, which was still feeding hard. It swept out from the darker water close to the boulder and the float simply daggered down. What a fight! A magnificent sight, this great creature boring and jagging towards the bottom, desperate to reach sanctuary. Sometimes it would be directly beneath my feet, only to power away again, across the current, trying to find sanctuary. Eventually it was netted, and I waded across the river again and took a quick photograph before returning a very fine barbel to the river.

Baits for Summer Barbel

Summer barbel baits fall into three categories, which for convenience we can call naturals, standards and particles. The first are my favourites and include lobworms, dead and live fish, leeches, caddis grubs and other insects – in fact all the things barbel are used to finding in the river in the natural way.

Well-tried offerings like cheese, cheese paste and luncheon meat are the main standards. Luncheon meat remains a killer bait and you can experiment with all sorts of different makes and flavours cut to different sizes. Peperami or similar sausage is also a useful addition to the range. It is also a good idea to experiment with the powder flavourings used for carp, as they really ring the changes by spicing up a meat bait. Fry a tin or two of meat in a couple of large tablespoons of each of the flavourings you want to try. The finished product will be a tasty version of the normal luncheon meat but with a tough, rough outer skin which fends off the attentions of minnows and gudgeon.

Then we have particles: hemp, sweetcorn, maggots, casters and tares. Personally, I favour the first two of these. Hemp remains a brilliant barbel attractor but it can be tricky to use and sometimes you will experience false bites. With sweetcorn there is the risk that barbel, through overfamiliarity, will quickly recognize it as a danger. However, in my experience they have to be under intense fishing pressure before corn sends out warning signals to them, and even then, you can easily dye corn red or orange and this will increase its life.

Despite these problems, there is no need to feel under great pressure when it comes to selecting barbel baits. Just choose two or three that you have confidence in and fish them intelligently in the right places and you're almost certain to succeed. My own favourite barbel bait? Well, taking a leaf from the traditionalists' book, I believe that in the low, clear water of summer nothing beats a large, lively and succulent lobworm.

The Snags

It was during a winter storm that the alder tree simply groaned and collapsed, taking with it the substantial section of the bank that was embraced by its roots. The stricken tree fell into what had always been a prime barbel swim and stayed there, its demise adding another attraction to an already popular place! Over the seasons the number of barbel attracted there grew and grew and, whenever conditions allowed, you could count on seeing fish in the area, sometimes lots of them.

So it was one summer's day as Roger and I stood watching. The barbel were in the upper part of the water, twisting in and out of the old dead branches. They were flashing frequently – very probably feeding on insects in and on the dead wood. They were also predating hard on small fry and minnows – of that surprising fact neither of us had any doubt whatever. From our positions, we could see fish after fish drive the minnows to the surface and then lunge into them – often so violently that they actually cleared the river by a foot or more.

With intense interest Roger watched the

There were those who didn't believe me when I said that I had seen barbel in big numbers so close to the surface in a fallen tree.
A photograph shows it all. There is no doubt that these fish were actively feeding and we must accept that barbel do not always feed off the bottom. In fact, a bait freelined or trotted in mid-water can often produce fish. See how many you can count in this one photograph.

Another shot of the same scene but this time a barbel is actually flashing: in fact it was scraping along one of the branches, sucking in attached insects and snails.

41

swim that day and the next. It would have been quite possible to have attacked the barbel in the 'snags', as other anglers had done in the past. But the problem with that approach was the strong chance of a fish breaking free. It was as though the barbel themselves knew this and chose the swim because of the confidence it gave them. Roger is not an angler to take risks with fine fish like these and he set about finding an alternative strategy.

The barbel were clearly there in numbers, and in the mood for feeding. Therefore the plan he devised was to lure them out of the bush into the shallower, clearer water just downstream, where he could attack them with a far better prospect of success. He embarked on a major baiting programme throughout the next day, introducing maggots, casters, hemp and grains of corn regularly, just upstream of the snags, so that

Roger watches intently, hands cupped around his Polaroids to cut out any shafts of light. I lost count of the hours that he lay there motionless, studying the barbel, beginning to learn their every move and watching as they picked up the scent of the bait and dropped off down-river to intercept it.

all manner of irresistible odours were given off as they trundled past.

One by one, the barbel began to peel away, out of the snags and down-river, looking for this bonanza of delectable goodies. By late afternoon almost all of them were gathered on the gravel, feeding hard, and that was when Roger set to work.

He waded into the river itself, well upstream and decided to try for the fish with a quivertip and feeder. He would hold the rod – a killing method when a swimfeeder is being used. There is no reason to assume that this set-up always calls for a rod rest, and in

Above: A barbel – the first of many that session – comes to the net. Notice how useful thigh-boots can be.

Right: The fish is held triumphantly for a couple of seconds in the sunlight. It was deep and powerful for a summer barbel: often after spawning they take time to build back to such prime condition.

fact holding the rod can be far neater and much more efficient. Every now and then you can move it minutely, here and there – just enough to induce a take. And when the take does come, you can hit it immediately, with confidence, knowing exactly what has been happening on the line.

The run of water in which the barbel were now feeding was rapid and this posed its own difficulties: the bait was coming out of the feeder quite quickly and rolling off down-river. The problem for Roger was that the hook bait, being tethered, would bounce around up and down on the bottom in a most unnatural fashion. So he shotted it right down to keep it hard on the gravel and to stop it rising and wavering as the fast water rushed over it. This was a crucial adjustment, for he had to get the barbel to regard the hook bait as food washed from the feeder. Two large shots 3in and 6in from the hook kept the bait hard on the bottom, as I could see from up the bank.

Roger caught his barbel, and landed every single one. The bites were real thumpers, the tussles incredible, but never was there any danger of him losing a fish and so perhaps inflicting injury. He displayed a valuable insight into how barbel feed and behave. In short, it rarely pays to go straight to a swim and start fishing with preconceived ideas – far better to take the time to work out the precise approach called for by the situation.

Low-water Tactics

In summer, when it has not rained for weeks, even on big rivers the gravel is exposed. The flow is thin and slow and the pools are constantly shallowing. But this does not mean that barbel have stopped feeding. A commonly heard excuse for failure with the species in summer is that their feeding spells are restricted, perhaps to the dead hours of darkness. But this is by no means always true,

Touch Legering

Throughout his fishing life the Master Angler is concerned with achieving as close a harmony with the fish as he possibly can. If you are fishing a river and looking at a quivertip for bites then you are dependent on the rod and not your own sense of touch. The rod is useful as an extension of you, but it is also a barrier between you and the fish. Touch legering, by contrast, brings you into the most immediate contact imaginable, and in my experience it's a particularly good method for pike. As for choice of rod for this species, it's best to use a 10–11ft model with largish rings that allow the line to pass through with minimal friction.

Find a comfortable position and cast out. Then align your rod as accurately as you can with the bait. Hold the rod in your usual hand, with support from a rod rest if necessary, and loop the line around the thumb and index finger of your other hand. There are various ways of doing this, so experiment until you find the one that for you is the most responsive to bites. But remember that your index finger is particularly sensitive and so it will need to be brought into play.

Your fingers will register all sorts of things when fishing like this – weed and rubbish against the line, fish moving the bait, fish bumping into the line and, of course, the pike themselves.

I simply don't have the space here to describe all the types of bite that you will feel. Try it and you will soon discover what I mean. You will do well to start on a swim where you know you will get lots of bites so that you can

gain practice and therefore confidence.

Touch legering is especially useful in summer, when a lot of fishing is done after dark. It's just as effective at night as it is by day, and there is no need for torches, isotopes or all the other clutter that can make night fishing such a trying business. You just sit there in the dark, feeling the line, alert and ready to set that hook!

The perfect touch-legering situation. The angler points the rod down-river towards the bait and is in perfect contact with a taking fish.

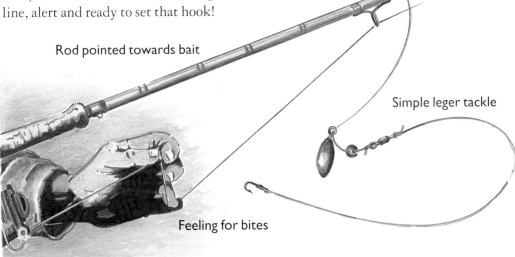

Rod pointed towards bait

Simple leger tackle

Feeling for bites

for barbel will feed day or night if you get the right bait to them in the right way.

Dawn is an excellent time to be out when the river is very low. Every good barbel angler knows this and makes that extra effort to be there before sunrise. At this hour barbel will still be feeding in the cloudy shallows, often with their backs out of the water, and most likely feeding very hard indeed. The main problem is that barbel are acutely aware of any potential predator when they are so vulnerable, and the crunch of boots on gravel will send them scurrying straight back to deeper water. And once one fish goes, the rest will follow.

For this reason real commando stuff is called for here. Look for your fish through binoculars and then approach them as circuitously as possible. Keep low, move very, very cautiously, try not to make a sound and don't lift your head high.

Get as close as you safely can to the group and then put a large natural bait in among them. It's wise to delay your first cast; meanwhile, look out for any fish that you fancy and note the route it is taking. This done, concentrate on making your first cast as precise as possible.

Two lobworms on a size 4 hook are excellent here, or a small dead fish such as a bullhead. If the water is really shallow you will probably need no weight at all, but if you are in doubt a single shot should do the trick. Watch the line very carefully where it enters

Below: The bare bones of the river show bleached in the summer sunshine. This can be a difficult time or, looked at from another point of view, it can be a period of immense possibilities. The big key is to watch hard and fish hard but approach every situation intelligently. All the old rules go out of the window in situations like this.

Above right: A fascinating shot of a big barbel disturbed in the shallows just after sun up. It was working along the margin, back out of the water, feeding hard on leeches, small fish and caddis grubs when I disturbed it by taking this photograph. Anyway, here is ample proof that this species ventures into very shallow water.

Below: This photograph is not as clear as I might have liked it but it still remains one of the most dramatic shots I have ever taken. Notice the large brown smear in the middle of the frame – thirty-five or forty barbel all writhing together like the snakes on Medusa's head! What you will see clearly is the fish in the lead, flashing as it feeds. Since this first sighting, I've seen several shoals behaving in exactly the same way – something I don't think I've ever read or heard reported before.

Above: Very frequently it pays to get into the river when the water is low because you have got to present a bait as naturally as you possibly can. You don't want to disturb the fish unnecessarily, so wade quietly, without scraping over the gravel.

Below: It's always a good idea to position a landing net close by unless you are quite sure that you can walk to the bank and draw the fish up into shallow water where it can often be unhooked without any need to lift it out.

the water and when it begins to tighten, strike at once. The fight will be explosive.

Being out and about in conditions like this can teach you an enormous amount. In fact, one of the most awe-inspiring sights I ever saw when barbel fishing was during a time of very low water.

I'd been looking for fish most of the day with very little luck, when I saw a slightly clouded area. I moved closer and really stared: the sight was quite extraordinary. There were thirty-five or forty barbel in front of me, in 6ft of water, and they were all enmeshed together, like sardines in a can. In fact, they formed just one large writhing body of fish. Occasionally one of them would flash and then they would all close up again.

This group of fish stayed together all the rest of the afternoon while I watched, moving slowly up and down the pool they had made their home. Fish hardly ever left this tight formation – except for just the odd one moving a couple of feet away before returning almost at once. The next day was the same and the day after that too. I began to see why action on a barbel swim when visibility is impossible can be so hectic one minute and totally dead the next. It is simply that the body of barbel has moved past your baited area and there is not one straggler left to give you sport.

Of course, catching these fish in such clear conditions was very easy. I simply put out a legered worm a couple of yards beyond them and then drew it slowly back among the group. The line would tighten and pull through my fingers within thirty seconds of each cast. I caught six or seven fish like this but I didn't really like it, because it was totally impossible to choose one above any other. There were some big barbel there, without doubt, but all I managed were fish of 5-7lb – not quite what I was after – so I left the group alone, grateful to them for the lesson they had taught me.

When the river is really low all sorts of stalking techniques can come into play and there are no hard-and-fast rules. Certainly, no book can cover every situation you are likely to meet. All you can do is study the water and decide on a plan of attack. The best thing is that in working it out for yourself you'll enjoy every minute of it.

However, there are times when it pays to stay at a known pool – for example, one where some big fish have been showing. Then you can really set up stall, quite confident that, with the water so low, the barbel won't move either upstream or downstream, but remain in front of you. Here you've just got to decide on a bait and a

This is the sort of sizeable pool where it can often pay to sit it out for a big fish you are fairly confident is present. A pool like this will often be partly cut-off from the rest of the river by very shallow runs both upstream and downstream and you can be fairly sure that a big fish is all but captive unless it takes it into its head to make a move – and that will probably be at night.

presentation that will fool them. It may be quite a while before they fall for it, because the water will perhaps be crystal-clear and very, very slow, so that they have a long time in which to make up their mind before deciding to suck in any bait.

Try small baits first – for example, two casters on a size 14 hook or three red maggots on a size 12. If this doesn't work or if the gudgeon and fry are a problem, try a shock approach: two lobworms on a size 2, or a thumb of sausage or even a large knob of breadflake. Don't always rely on a swimfeeder in slow pools, because the barbel will certainly be aware of the trick. A straight lead could well be better. Also, in the slack current, a catapulted bait will fall with a certain predictability.

All-night fishing is often a good tactic in times of low water. The fish will move after dark, around 10pm, say, and will feed quite hard until dawn, around 5am. You'll find that those seven hours pass quickly, with bites probably reaching a climax between 10.30pm and midnight.

Chub Stalking

When small rivers are down to their bare bones, and there is no more than a trickle of water from one pool to another, you realize that chub have not only the biggest eyes but also the most unwavering intelligence of any of our fishes.

Ben had seen a really big chub under a tree – a five-pounder at least – and it seemed to be up for the catching. He crossed the river about 100 yards upstream and then, on his knees, approached the best casting position. Quite confident of a take, he was going to freeline a large worm down to the fish.

But that chub had gone. It seemed uncanny. How on earth could it have known that Ben was planning an assault

In a shallow pool like this, floating crust can often be a really winning bait. Notice how this angler is approaching very cautiously and kneeling a couple of yards back from the water's edge, keeping low all the time.

Ben crosses the shallow river to get to the opposite bank and a position that will give him much better access to a big fish. If you can, never be afraid to criss-cross a river like this because catching chub in such situations is almost like a game of chess and you've got to manoeuvre for the best possible position.

Always approach a big chub on your knees! It's quite extraordinary the power of their vision – they have to be constantly aware of both food below them and predators above and behind.

on it? I'd watched the whole thing: Ben's approach had been perfect. It's as though very big chub have a sixth sense, and we can't afford to forget this.

On tiny pools it pays to move on your belly, and begin fishing right back from the water's edge. Surprisingly, even on a small, shallow pool chub will come up for floating crust. But be careful: it's all too easy to snatch at your strike and miss the fish. Everything is so close and so intense, and your heart is beating so wildly, that you can easily make a mistake. Just keep your cool and take your time, and wait for the line to move.

A long rod is the best choice here because you can keep the amount of line on the water to a minimum and mend any sign of drag at once. If the river is small enough, you can avoid laying any line on the surface at all, and this is particularly useful when the chub are very spooky.

Floating crust is often a winner, as Gerry, another young angler, was to discover. He'd done a fair bit of scouting up and down the stream and, from high up on some rocks, he could see a good fish or two moving in the pool below.

He took his time and fed crusts into the water upstream so that they dawdled down into the pool and wafted around in the slow, oily current. Soon the odd chub

began to cock an eye at this food on the surface and the occasional lazy take was made. Gerry just kept trickling those crusts through, never losing patience, never getting frustrated, but instead slowly building up the fishes' confidence.

With his first cast, one of the biggest chub approached, cautiously, but obviously with serious intent. It took the crust without making a bulge in the water – the surface just dimpled. In fact, if Gerry hadn't been sitting 12ft higher, directly above it, he wouldn't have seen a thing. Moreover, the line hardly moved: the chub just sat there below the surface with the bread in its mouth. Again, Gerry played it cool, waited ten seconds and only as the fish began to sink from sight did he strike. Yet, despite all his care, it was only just hooked on the outside of the lips and the hook fell out once it hit the net.

This is not unusual at all with clear-water chub, and the more you stalk chub the more

A fascinating shot of a chub gently taking a piece of floating crust. We often think of chub really going hard at a floating bait but this is not always the case by any means and sometimes they will simply sip even a big bait from the surface with barely any commotion whatsoever.

often you'll witness them running a yard or more with the bait on the outside of the lips before they take it in. I shan't speculate why this is but it can be partially overcome by using a livebait that doesn't submit so easily. Crayfish were excellent for this – although they are too rare to use nowadays – but *live* minnows and really frail wriggling lobworms have much the same effect.

I'm convinced that the reason why so many clear-water chub bites are missed by anglers fishing the quivertip is that you just can't give line and delay the strike till the bait goes right in. Luckily, a lively, struggling bait can prove a godsend.

Above: Gerry has climbed down this steep bank to get right above his fish. Mind you, he is pressed in on his ledge, making sure his head doesn't protrude over the skyline and scare the fish. Notice also his drab clothing.

Above: Playing a chub from a 'bird's nest' position. The advantage of this is that you have great control over the fish, being directly above it, but on occasion the hook-hold can be weakened by this vertical pull. It pays to get the fish to the net as quickly as possible.

Left: Gerry looks rightly proud of a well-earned fish.

Chub on the Top

The greatest all-round feeders in our rivers, chub are aware of baits on the bottom, in mid-water and on the surface. In fact, it's on the top that many a big chub falls, largely because, with so few anglers now using the method, the fish are not so wary of it.

Provided the river is not heavily surface-fished, simply break up pieces of crust, throw them into midstream and follow them along the bank until the chub begin to hit at them. Now cast out into the commotion a matchbox-sized piece of crust on a size 4 hook and greased line. Takes are almost guaranteed, but do give a fish time to take a big piece of flake right in, especially if it is not well soaked.

So far so good, but the Master Angler will always be aware that chub will quickly wise up to your floating bread. It's then that you need to come up with minor variations that will continue to fool the fish. The diagrams below revolve around rigs that retain the floating crust but introduce slowly sinking flake as a

hook bait. The idea is that while the chub may have begun to look cautiously at the crust on the surface, they will view a sinking piece of flake with total confidence, probably assuming that it has broken off from the crust above.

These methods, which have all caught chub, show how an inventive approach can get round some of the problems posed by this clever species.

Chub take floating crust in various ways, sometimes splashing at it and at other times sucking it in with barely a ripple.

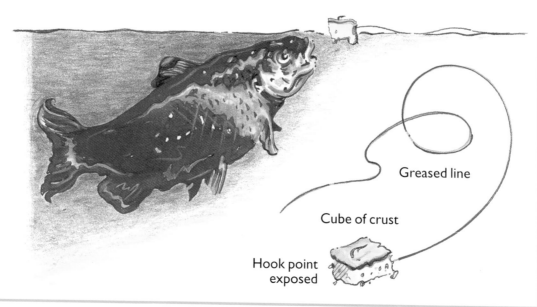

Greased line

Cube of crust

Hook point exposed

Roach Approach

My childhood friends and I always felt like tearing our hair out when we were fishing clear canals in summer and could see the roach milling around taking every single item of food but those on a hook. We just couldn't understand it. A thousand maggots would all disappear – all bar one: the one wriggling on a size 18 hook. How on earth did they know? How could they spot the betrayal so consistently?

I still don't know the answer, not after decades of watching and thinking about it. In fact, my admiration for clear-water roach has risen massively over the intervening years. You've got to be very clever to force them into making a mistake.

I remember seeing one big fish come in and out of deep water, moving back and forth over a clear piece of sand that was baited up with bread, time after time, over an eight-hour period, and only taking one mouthful on each visit. I took that fish eventually but my bait had been in the water for three hours before the float finally trembled and sat up. And that wasn't until it was half-dark!

Again, one sunny day in August I saw a tempting group of roach in very clear water. I waded out some yards above them, watching very carefully and beginning to dribble in bait. I began with maggots, just to get them to look for food and to put aside a little of their caution. Soon, a group of fish – about twenty in all, including some sizeable ones – were beginning to feed with a sort of controlled frenzy. This was when I began to make my move.

I continued to feed in maggots but also introduced pinches of breadflake every now and again to see the reaction of the fish.

Even for roach you can wade if you take a great deal of care not to disturb the swim. However, roach are more wary than barbel and certainly react immediately to any scraping of the gravel.

Look at these roach, totally oblivious to the maggots floating past them: even quick and aware fish like these take time to switch on to a food source.

At last! One of the
roach turns sharply
sideways to
intercept a maggot
and you know that
the feeding spree
has begun.

Main picture: An
underwater shot of
roach making use of
what weed cover
there is – typical of
the species. Find
weed and you will
often find roach.

A really well-rounded and heavy summer roach – a truly magnificent creature.

These, thankfully, were taken as well. The importance of the flake is that it is much easier to present on a hook than a single maggot. You can actually pinch it on in a very fluffy state and this will counteract any weight and make it fall as naturally as any free offering. With fish like this, your presentation has to be perfect as possible.

The rod was a 13ft trotting rod and the line 2lb b.s. straight through to the hook. There was no float, just a small shot nipped on about 6in above the hook to give me a little control and to help me place the bread exactly where I wanted it.

I felt sure that there was little or no chance that a fish would accept the bait on the drop, so I wanted to manoeuvre it quickly onto a piece of swaying weed. On the third attempt I succeeded. The fish were moving backwards and forwards over and under the weed and there was my pinch of flake neatly tethered, awaiting inspection. The first fish to see it simply altered its position in the water, went

down head first and the flake was gone. What a beautiful fish. Of course, landing it spooked the rest. But then on small summer rivers like this you usually get only one chance and if you blow that you've blown everything.

Canals in Summer

Locating fish on canals is one of the major problems in angling – except during those times in the winter when the fish come together in great groups that become well known. In the summer it is often a particularly difficult task.

Here flexibility is, as always, a major key: it never pays to settle for the first swim vacant next to the point of access. When I think back to the anglers that I have known to be successful on canals, mobility has been an important component of each one's skill. These anglers are happy to keep moving about on canals, but what are the features that they're looking for?

Reedbeds are often a major factor, especially earlier in the summer when tench and carp are still in the spawning mood. On

Reading the Quivertip

The quivertip will doubtless remain one of the best ways to detect a bite. But because it can behave in confusing ways, it's quite possible to miss seeing a bite altogether and end up striking wildly at nothing more than a piece of passing weed!

When a fish is attacking a bait, the tip's movements are erratic and quick and positive; somehow it looks alive. But if weed or rubbish is to blame, very often the tip will pull round slowly, moving with the speed of the current in a ponderous fashion. You can be pretty sure it's not a fish on the end!

When it pulls round heavily for no clear reason, the fish, usually a barbel or chub, has simply taken the bait and wheeled off into sanctuary with it. The fish will probably be on when you strike. Other movements can be more difficult to explain. What about the sudden bang all the way down the rod that comes out of nowhere? Possibly a line bite, possibly a fish picking up the bait and dropping it. Leave the rod alone and a better bite may well materialize in a minute or so.

What about a series of tremors that takes the tip round a very slight amount? A small fish could be to blame, pulling and pecking at the bait, or it could be one brushing against the line, occasionally nosing the bait, unsure of what to do. On a very few occasions it could be a very confident fish taking the bait well into its mouth and not moving off, possibly even inching around the swim looking for other foodstuffs. What do you do? Well, nine times out of ten it's best to leave the rod and wait for something better to develop. If nothing does, then start hitting some of the more dramatic twitches.

The real worry is that a confident fish could swallow the bait and cut the line with its throat teeth – something neither of you will be happy about. If this happens once, you can make allowance for the fact that the fish are already in there feeding confidently on the bait, and start to strike much sooner. Alternatively, move the lead or the swimfeeder much closer to the bait so that the fish feels resistance a lot earlier, moves off and gives a confident bite.

Quivertips are a wonderful tool, but they do need to be interpreted correctly. Don't just sit there waiting for that unmissable bite. The tip is sending out a stream of messages and it's up to you to read them as accurately as you can.

A sturdy rod rest is essential with two rods used at long range.

disused canals especially, the reedbeds may be extensive and may be the focal point for fish from miles around. Even if the canal is used by boat traffic, smaller reedbeds could prove equally effective as hot-spots. And the boats themselves aren't always bad news! One that's been anchored for some time may well have become a particularly useful feature for fish seeking shelter from the sun.

Locks – used and unused – often provide another summer gathering point – especially when freshwater is cascading down, giving a dash of oxygen to what is generally stale water. Any feeder streams provide the same sort of bonus, since fish are always looking for new, invigorating water.

Of course, ambush can work, especially if you get to the canal early and put down bait where you are confident that fish will be passing. For this approach, an area just upstream or downstream of a bridge may prove ideal, as will perhaps the fringes of a

Right: Even small locks like this can provide a great deal of oxygen for the water in a dry summer.

turning basin. Most species do move along canals during the night and if you have any clues at all where they're heading, then be there at daybreak.

First light is very important for the summer canal fisherman. Many canals are busy places and if they are fairly narrow and shallow there is very little sanctuary for the fish during daylight. Night is the only lengthy period when they can feel secure. Fishing at first light allows you to cash in on this false sense of security that they have developed. It's also an excellent time to see fish moving. If you can choose a swim that gives you a good view along the canal, keep scanning constantly with binoculars to see if there is any surface activity.

On most canals it's almost impossible to overestimate the fishes' need for security, so

Featureless banks make boats even more desirable to fish: they like them for the shade and protection they give and even the anchor ropes will attract canal perch.

A bridge, a boat, a sunken fence and overhanging trees — all fish-holding features on a canal.

investigate any feature that could offer sanctuary. For example, many fish hole up on the far side of turning basins, particularly if there's no easy access to the area from the towpath. Far-side trees are also excellent – especially, once again, if there's no footpath on that bank. If the trees have fallen in the water here and there, so much the better, for sunken branches often collect a great number of fish around them, particularly in broad daylight. Perhaps, in some hidden corner of the canal, there may be a few water lilies growing; it doesn't need to be an extensive mat of them – just a few stems will provide the security that a group of roach will seek.

On many summer canals distance can be an important consideration and the further that you are prepared to walk or cycle away from the normal access points, the greater your chances of coming across good fish. Frequently, big roach, especially, will move as far away as they can from built-up areas. If there are out-of-town stretches with perhaps gardens leading down to the far bank, then these are well worth trying – not just in the summer but at any time of the year.

Summer evenings are often another golden period on the canal: when the light is hovering, about to give way to darkness. Then even the suburban canal can become a magical place, full of mystery and expectation. Roach, in particular, respond to this last light and you will often see them becoming active as the sun goes down. Stirring seriously for the first time in twelve or fourteen hours, they come out of hiding and start to search for food. They are again catchable, so it's a good idea to fish on, after darkness, with an isotope in the float. Bites will be surprisingly bold and then, as the roach begin to move away, very often bream will start to move in. Now is also the time for an encounter with the odd passing carp – another species that nearly always prefers to travel along canals under cover of darkness.

Left: A perfect canal roach. It was taken by laying on with half a lobworm in the calm of dawn.

Below: The scene is set for a canal ambush. Choose a place that fish might visit at night – reedbeds or a turning basin or anything that provides a feature.

Laying-on

The credit for the laying-on method is usually given to the Taylor brothers, who fished tench lakes systematically in the 1950s. Their idea was to set the float a couple of feet over-depth, put all the shot on the bottom 18in from the hook, then reel tight until the float is half-cocked. A taking tench will then cause the float to either lie flat or slide straight under.

However, putting all the shot at the bottom can lead to tench becoming wary and rejecting baits unless they are sucking boldly. It is probably better to put quite a bit of shot, or even most of it, between the bottom shot and the float. This makes the hook and bait react more naturally, and more tench and bream are hooked safely. An excellent float-fishing method with larger baits especially, laying-on should never have become as neglected as it is today.

While the young learn the basic skills of fishing, some older anglers rediscover lost ones, such as laying-on.

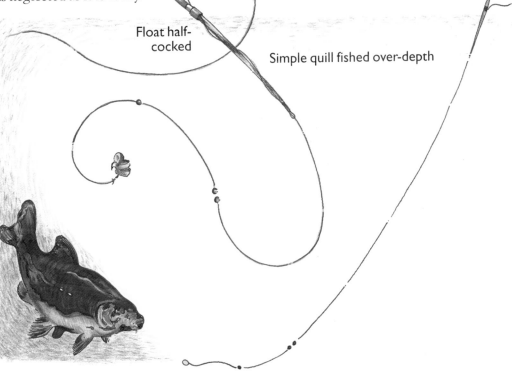

Float half-cocked

Simple quill fished over-depth

Summer Stillwaters

—— Carp in the Reedbeds ——

It was a typical day for me, walking through the park where I live, past the lake to the gatehouse. And, as usual, I made a major detour round to the far side of the water, where the reedbeds crowd out across the shallows. Invariably sixty to seventy percent of the fish are in this reed area during the average summer day. However, ninety-five percent of the anglers who fish the lake are anywhere but close to the reeds. It seems that fish and reeds go together, whereas reeds and anglers most certainly don't.

It would be easy to miss the very large fish lying in the shade at the top of this picture – in fact I nearly did. When you are water-watching you've really got to scrutinize every part of the swim because you can fail to spot something special.

It's obvious why fish frequent reedbeds so much during the heat of the day. There they find sanctuary from all predators: bird, mammal, bigger fish, or man. Reedbeds also offer food. Pull up a reed stem and you will be amazed at the number of snails on the vegetation itself and the bloodworms in the roots. Insects of all kinds colonize reedbeds because the water there, being warmer and more stable than in open stretches, ideally suits their fragile life patterns.

That day there were a good number of unremarkable fish everywhere: bream and small common carp or, possibly, wild carp – the difference between the two has become blurred. Then, in a tiny piece of open water I saw *it* – a wild carp (let's call it that) that was at least twice the normal size for the lake. It was a superb fish and I watched it up close for a long while, as I plotted my approach. I had

Above: The fish leave the swim – as usual in convoy, head-to-tail in a long line. This is very typical with wild carp, whereas mirrors will move around in a broader group.

Below: The fish stopped off in shallow water just beneath a boy's rod. Ill at ease, one grabbed a bait and bolted off with it before, not surprisingly, moving on.

Always try to make the best possible use of long grasses where they occur around a water. Camouflage is extremely important if you are fishing very close into the margins. It's quite uncanny how aware carp can be of a human presence on a previously deserted water and for this reason you shouldn't take any chances.

no tackle with me, nor was I sure what bait I had back at the house, but I was convinced I could find something.

After about an hour the big carp, like the two smaller ones accompanying it, showed signs of restlessness. Their eyeballs began to move more frequently and their pectorals began to stir up the dust of the bottom – sure signs that they were awakening from a summer siesta.

The big fish leading, they moved from their small bay and into the channel, where a boy was fishing. They picked up a few bits of loose bait around his float but were obviously nervous. They could see his rod extending over the water and his line, to them, was

like rope. After a few mouthfuls, they were off and I knew exactly where they were heading. About fifty yards down the channel, another large bay opened out, once again surrounded by reeds, and I knew this was a favourite place for late-afternoon feeding.

I ran the half a mile home and grabbed a rod, a reel, a couple of floats, hooks, some shot and a landing net. But what would I do for bait? Rummaging in the larder, I found a can of red kidney beans. Excellent. Back to the lake I raced. As I had guessed, there the fish were, feeding – not hard, but feeding all the same. Hiding behind the reedbeds, hardly daring to breathe, I catapulted out a single kidney bean at a time until about fifteen lay in a large area in the bay in front of me. I knew that it was no good concentrating the beans, because the fish weren't feeding in a determined way at all. All they were doing was moseying around, tipping up and sipping in the odd mouthful here and there.

Again I watched. The fish were now only five or so yards away from me and the water

Above: Perfect! The typical signs of a carp feeding in a tight, controlled fashion. Look at those close bubbles rising to the surface.

Below: A shallow landing net is no use at all in situations like this, because once the carp is over the rim you don't want any mistakes to occur.

A typical carp – still quite lean after spawning. The bait that brought about its downfall lies on the net above it.

was crystal-clear. One bean was taken, then another and then the fish I had set my sights on, took three in five minutes. It was time to make a cast.

I have no doubt that the big fish saw my bean – all its movements indicated so – but I am equally certain that it saw the float. Twice it came in towards the bean but then veered away when it was about a yard off. It just had to be the float that was spooking it, because around the lake there must have been at least thirty anglers, most of them sitting watching their bobbing floats – warning beacons to a wily old fish.

I reeled in and looked around. Geese had been sheltering overnight at my feet and there, hallelujah! lay a large white feather. I tied it on 6ft above the bean and cast out again, although casting was now more difficult, because of the feather's wind resistance. Nevertheless, I reached the mark, and sat back to await events, peering through the reed stems.

Once, one of the smaller fish came in to take the bean and I removed it quickly. Back it went. Then the big fish came close ... and even closer ... then right over the bean and off with it. Luckily, the feather had aroused absolutely no terrors and soon I was looking down at my largest-ever wildie.

Carp are not alone in displaying this wariness of floats, for often I've seen tench in clear water shy away from even a small, clear-bodied one. And if a fish can see a float so clearly and know that it spells trouble, then very probably the line cutting at an angle through the water also sends out shock-waves, especially if it is in a swim with little mid-water weed.

These are very important considerations, for they can make all the difference between catching and not catching fish. If you have any suspicions at all that it is the float or the angle of the line that is causing problems, it makes sense to leger or freeline. But do make sure that the terminal tackle is all hard on the bottom and therefore less obvious to any passing fish.

When you consider the awareness that fish have of what is happening in their immediate environment, it makes you think of the disturbance we cause when we reel a bait in quickly. Again, in clear water, I've seen shoals of roach, crucian carp and tench appear quite agitated when the bait is retrieved noisily. As long as you're fishing in the right place with the right bait – that golden rule again – it's wise to leave the bait out as long as it is practical and then, when you have to retrieve it, do so as gently as you can.

Even when you are using an umbrella or a bivvy it is still quite possible to become one with the bankside. Position everything thoughtfully, using every scrap of cover that you can. Of course, on a really pressured lake it is not so important, but if you are out in the wilds then your presence will certainly be noted by the fish.

The Long-stay Session

Nowadays many carp, tench and bream specialists concentrate on stints that last for a week or more. The long session has become part of the conventional doctrine on big fish. Not that it doesn't work: the problem is simply that very often the process becomes stereotyped. The angler – and I've done this myself – simply arrives, sets up for a long stay, then casts out his baits and settles back for what he knows will feel like an eternity. He will probably have with him all manner of things to divert him while waiting for a big fish to come along, take his bait and make his day.

Long sessions were not always like this. In the 1950s, when this type of fishing began, a totally different mentality predominated. The forgotten truth is that the long stay is one of the best ways to merge with the environment. The angler would, by being at the waterside for forty-eight or seventy-two hours, hopefully begin to understand all its rhythms and get to know intimately the water and the fishes' movements. Then, the

What long-stay fishing is all about — the angler merging with the surroundings.

If you are quiet you will find that nature continues around you unalarmed. Never think for a moment that fish don't pick up the vibes from waterfowl – they do. Alarm swans and you will alert the lake.

long-stay angler was constantly active – when not sleeping, of course – and regarded every hour as a challenge, not time to be spent reading or watching a portable TV! By contrast, there are still plenty of men who spend a long time by the water who understand this older concept. These are the men who have the gift of blending into the mists or becoming as natural as a bough of a waterside tree.

I recognize that on some modern waters where there is a lot of noise and activity, this sort of concealment is not so important. But on more natural waters camouflage can prove vital. Carp, in particular, are very often more concerned about bankside activity than they are about lines and terminal tackle, and provided you do not arouse their suspicions in the first place, a take is often a possibility even on fairly crude tackle.

The beauty of a long session on a quiet water is that you can pick your swim after a great deal of thought. Plan exactly where you want to put your baits and the game is at least half won. The more you get to know the water, watch the fish and recognize their patrol routes and feeding areas, the better your chances. Even an entire day just spent watching is never wasted if it helps you to identify exactly the right area to bait up.

It's almost impossible to specify what this area might look like, since hot-spots differ widely from water to water. But if there is one give-away, then it is a clear, shining area on the lake or pit bed where the silt has been cleaned away and the sand or gravel looks like it has been hoovered. In most cases it will have been – by the fish!

You've found a spot that you are totally happy with, you've probably seen fish there tipping up to feed, and perhaps some bubbles have risen. Whatever the clues, you know that you are in the right area. Now it's time to think about the bait and presentation. Is it a bait that you are happy with and have confidence in? Do you think the fish will quickly recognize it as food? Once you've decided about the bait, stick with it for at least the rest of the session.

Above: Look at that white shirt – it stands out a mile! However, the position is a good one for a long-stay session since it commands as much of the lake as possible.

Below: A tremendous fish and a just reward for a long-stay session. Interestingly, this carp was taken at dawn on a stalking rod – a skill that should never be neglected.

Particles

The term 'particles' simply describes bait in the form of multiple small food items – maggots, casters, hempseed, peanuts, sweetcorn and so on. The use of particles as we now understand the term began with the new approach to carp fishing in recent decades. Of course, roach fishermen have used particles since the beginning of time! Sweetcorn was the first of the modern particle baits, but many others, in particular nuts and seeds, are now used.

One of these, hempseed, is especially effective as a carpet bait, allowing you to present many other baits on top of it. Of the many ways to prepare hempseed the best is simply to boil the seeds until they begin to open and show the white kernel inside. Then simply turn down the heat and let them simmer. Leave them in hot water overnight and they should be fine

for the next day. Don't worry if you don't use all the hempseed in one go during a long session – prolonged heat will only make it become more sticky and smelly, and so irresistible!

You can lay a carpet of hempseed either by hand close in or, further out, with bait droppers or swimfeeders, or a catapult. If boats are allowed, it is hard to beat going out to a marker and tipping the stuff over the side from a bucket.

All sorts of particles can be used over hempseed to great effect, including mini-boilies in their many varieties. Luncheon meat is a favourite of mine, as are casters and even maggots or half a lobworm or a couple of brandlings. The aim is to pull the fish in with the hempseed, keep them feeding and then present a slightly larger bait that they can't resist.

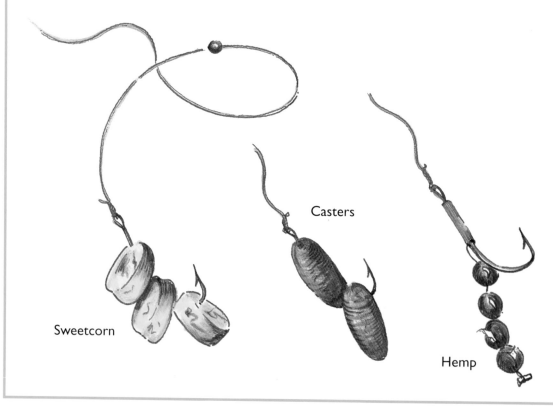

Sweetcorn

Casters

Hemp

A single hempseed can also be used as a bait itself. Simply superglue one to a hair or firm it into a small ball round a bogey!

Bloodworm, the larva of the gnat, has generally been seen as the bait of the matchman. But these tiny, gyrating little worms, which can be bought from some tackle shops or collected from streams and ponds, also make an effective particle bait.

Simply compress a handful into a mixture of clay or loam to which some brown-crumb groundbait has been added, and throw the ball into the swim. You will find that the groundbait takes the bloodworm down to the bottom, and then explodes into a nice cloud. The bloodworm then take over, leaping and gyrating a few inches in the bottom zone. Inevitably, very small fish are attracted, but so are large carp, tench and bream – and probably every species present in that water. It's quite possible to create mayhem in a swim using bloodworm.

The question is what to use as hookbait, since bloodworm are not at all easy to thread onto either hook or a hair and can be pulled apart in seconds by hordes of ravenous little fish. It's probably easier to try a small brandling or two, again on a hook or on a hair, or a tiny redworm. This approach is not often used but can work well, so experiment until it pays off for you.

A long-stay session encapsulated – a happy, relaxed angler holding a really beautiful fish.

Now go for the simplest presentation that you think will work on that water with those fish. There are all manner of complex rigs described in magazines and books these days, and ninety percent of them are totally superfluous. Even some of the anglers who have devised them are prepared to admit as much privately. So keep your set-up simple, and then there will be much less chance of getting it wrong.

Another key tactic is to keep all your options open. For example, while you might have unshakeable confidence in the baited area out in front of you, it still pays to have binoculars by your side and scan the water frequently. Also, each time you reel in, take an hour or even two hours out, depending on the size of the water, to walk slowly around it, watching carefully.

Go equipped with a stalking rod that you have already made up. This should be around 11ft long, with a test curve of about 2lb. If you're after carp, 10lb line should suffice for most situations, and have a float, a hook and a small container of natural baits to hand. As you wander, with a net slung round your back, look out for any movement in the marginal reeds and sunken bushes. Tread carefully, like a Red Indian, and you will be surprised at how many fish you see drifting in and out with feeding on their mind.

There are many delights attached to the long session – the satisfaction of knowing a plan has worked out, the excitement of stalking a big fish in lily beds, the sheer joy of sunbathing by a beautiful lake on a wonderful summer's day. And no less exciting is the knowledge that, with dusk about to fall, the owls will hoot from the wood and a fox may come grubbing around the bank to see if bait has been left for its supper. At its best, the long-stay session can be the pinnacle of fishing, seeing the angler become one with nature again – exactly what fishing, like all forms of hunting, was for our distant ancestors.

When you get tench switched on to particles, more than other baits, you will find that they come thick and fast. After you've spent ages waiting for a shoal to arrive, four or five fish can fall within half an hour, so be prepared.

Thoughts on Tench

A strange thing about tench is that many anglers regard them as an old-fashioned fish, a species that somehow hasn't caught up with modern times. That's why you often see anglers sitting round a tench lake trying for them in time-honoured ways – with big baits fished hard on the bottom – and hardly ever a bite to show for it.

Much of the old advice still works, it's true – especially when it comes to pre-baiting, and even raking a swim (where possible), but it is on the question of presentation that a lot of rethinking is needed. Somehow, in waters right across their distribution range, tench started to feed in a 'modern' way. As a result, we're looking at a whole population of careful tench, of suckers and blowers, rather than the gobblers of the past! I remember when a tench would come along, tip up and, if the

food item failed to rise to its suck, pick it up with its lips. That is rarely the case now, which is why so many large tethered baits sit unmolested session after session.

So why does the bait fail repeatedly to rise into the mouth of the sucking tench, sending so many sad anglers home fishless? The reason is partly the weight of the hook, of the line even, and of the shot – all factors that make the small but vital difference between a bite or rejection.

But are there any new options? Well, some anglers advocate very light tackle. This means confronting tench with almost match-type gear, and I've done it myself on occasion when I've been at my wits' end. The problem is that you can end up playing a huge fish in weedy water on 2lb line and a size 18 hook. It's a nightmare for you and the fish, so it's not an approach I personally recommend.

Probably the best way to catch wary tench these days is to use a balanced bait. For example, if you are using grains of sweetcorn, simply pop a piece of polystyrene foam between the two grains on the hook to counterbalance their weight. You will find that the hook and the bait hover on the bottom, ready to rise as soon as the tench begins to suck.

Test this set-up at home in the sink before fishing. The important thing is to be sure of just how much foam you need. (If you wish to put your mind completely at rest, paint the foam the colour of the bait you are using, though in practice this is seldom necessary.) Experiment with the set-up. For example, if you are using three casters on a size 14 hook make sure that two of those casters are floaters and you will find that the whole outfit is, once again, nicely counterbalanced and ready to rise at a moment's notice!

If you don't want to make the bait float, then you can make the hook buoyant instead by supergluing a sliver of cork or polystyrene onto it – a fiddly procedure, but well worthwhile. Again, test this out at home to ensure complete precision. Obviously, the heavier the bait and the bigger the hook the more buoyancy will have to be added to the hook's shank. This sounds a painstaking process but it's not difficult and it makes a tremendous difference.

The hair-rig is seen by some anglers as a tool of the carp fisherman alone, but this is wrong. Hairs have radically improved barbel sport, and are certainly valued in tench fishing. You might find that you have to use a shorter hair for tench than you would for carp, simply because everything is scaled down. My advice is, begin with a hair of around ½in and then, if you are missing bites, vary the length. Often, having the bait a tiny distance off the hook makes all the difference – even if it's only ⅛in. Yet on occasion I've had resounding success with a 1in hair.

In clear water, if you're lucky, you will see the whole fascinating process unfold. You will see tench come into the swim, tip up over food and begin to suck, their mouths some 1-2in from the bottom. Untethered food will rise easily and be swallowed. Food that does not rise for any reason will be shunned and left to rot. It's this type of awareness that sets the Master Angler just that little bit apart.

I'm not suggesting here a parallel between tench and the high-tech world of carp fishing. Tench simply aren't like carp. You can still fish for them with a float, by reedbeds, in the same old ways – provided at all times you think about what is happening in the swim, down towards the bottom, where the action is taking place. Work out what the tench is doing down there: why, for example, if it's bubbling and blowing, your float isn't dipping. You'll always find a reason if you are prepared to understand the world of the fish and to experiment.

Who can resist the challenge of a fish like this?

An angler in the water nets a really huge barbel caught just before the weather breaks. These golden periods are really warm and welcoming and the fish feed very hard in quite shallow, streamy runs of water.

Autumn

We talk about autumn, but the American word 'fall' conveys better what autumn is all about: falling leaves, falling rain and falling temperatures. In fact, it's a time when all our waters are in a state of flux after having been largely stable for the previous three to five months. Often the change in the weather can come with dramatic suddenness. September and even early October can offer warm, mild, sunny days when insects swarm and swallows still skim the pool in the evening.

Then one morning you wake up to find grey skies, cold winds and icy rain stair-rodding down. The halcyon days of summer seem to be gone for ever. Water temperatures can drop 2.75°C (5°F) in a day, and rivers can swell to double their size in the same period. Weed begins to die and trundle in the current or foul the bottom of stillwaters. Leaves are everywhere, blown from the trees by the sharp, icy blast, clogging your line, congregating in eddies, building up on the bottom in slacks and putting fish off the feed. As the forces of nature show their more violent side, fish are pulled and pushed here and there all over the water system.

But it's not all bad news for the angler at this time of the year. In their own way, many fish species also realize that winter is coming and this provokes them into spells of heavy feeding. This is especially noticeable in carp, roach, barbel and bream, and even tench and crucians will feed harder and longer into the autumn than most anglers realize. These are great perch days too, especially as summer algae blooms clear in the colder water. Now the shoals of fingerlings are increasingly conspicuous and the perch begin to roam the water more and more aggressively, making the most of new opportunities.

Autumn Rivers

Trotting

There is often a golden period before the first frosts and floods. The river is still warm and still clear – almost like a summer river in many respects, but the fish are aware that the shorter, cooler nights have set in and that winter is on its way.

It's this knowledge that spurs barbel and chub into a spell of very hard feeding. They seek food in earnest at this time of year, and if you look hard enough you will see them ranging over the gravels. Time spent walking the banks and watching carefully is essential, and the signs to look·out for are flashes on the gravel, occasional rolling and dark, log-like shapes. You may see fish boil on the surface as a bird flies over, or a heron may clumsily take off at your approach – there are lots of little things that reveal the presence of fish, so it pays to give the water your full attention during these walks.

Once you think you have found fish – or at least a promising area where the water pushes steadily over a nice clean bottom – you need to work out how best to present a bait. Very often the answer will be a float. If you are fishing a big river you may well need to wade if you are going to present the bait absolutely ideally on your float set-up. If you have to

Possibly the most ideal time of the fishing year is the early autumn, particularly on days like the one seen here – mild, sunny and dry. You will tend to find that fish feed much harder now than they will in the summer or in the coming hard weather.

wade, then do so – provided the depths are quite safe (see page 22). Sometimes you might even be lucky and spot an exposed rock or even a tree trunk in mid-river that you can sit on or use as a bait table.

When wading, don't take too much with you. Apart from reliable thigh boots or chest waders, all you need is a bag slung over your shoulder with the bait in. Any spare hooks, floats, shot and so on can go in your pockets.

A 12ft rod is ideal and, while a centrepin reel is a joy to handle, a fixed-spool will do for nearly all occasions. You will probably need line of 3-6lb b.s., depending on the species you're after and the amount of snags.

As for the float, the choice is between a stick float for use close in and an Avon-style design for fishing quicker water at distance. Since the float is the key element, give careful thought to the following factors. First, it *must*

be clearly visible. Choose a colour that stands out against the colours on the river surface. If you're fishing under bright sky, a white float, for example, will be of little use, although it might come into its own in the shadow of dense overhanging branches or a rock.

Think also about the range at which you want to fish. If the water is shallow and clear, obviously you can't approach the fish closely and you'll have to trot for some distance to avoid spooking the shoal. A large float is best in this sort of long-trotting – you just can't follow the progress of a small float, so that it could be down and up again before you've moved a muscle.

Consider also how deep and fast the swim is, because the float must be able to take the amount of weight necessary to get the bait

down to the fish. A small float, lightly shotted, is likely to carry a bait swirling way over their heads. Most new trotters make the mistake of using too light a float. It's easy to think that a big float will somehow be off-putting, but to most fish it isn't. Provided it's properly weighted and balanced, a big float is just as sensitive as a small one, and much easier to control.

Once you're in the water, steadily feed down the line. This will gather fish in and

You cannot spend too much time walking and looking for fish. Always travel light and make sure there's nothing too heavy around your neck. Also be especially careful that your boots fit well – if they're too tight or too loose then rubbing and blisters are bound to occur.

The glory of autumn – here Robert is trotting for chub and barbel on a far-bank swim.

Trotting Skills

Since trotting is all about controlling the float and the bait beneath it, you must start off with the right rod. In most circumstances this should be 12–13ft long – anything shorter will almost certainly limit your ability to move the line delicately around on the water. The rod should be light because you'll have to hold it most of the day. It should also have a strong, accurate action, because when long-trotting you will often need to pick up line thirty or even eighty yards of line and set the hook into a sizeable fish.

The choice of reel is up to you. Centrepins have been prized for trotting over a century, and an angler who can control one is well on his way to becoming a master trotter. But the centrepin isn't the easiest reel to use, and you may prefer the fixed-spool. You won't find it as sensitive, but it's pretty well up to any trotting job that you may want to do.

As for the line, the most important thing is to make sure that it floats, even if this means giving it a light coating of

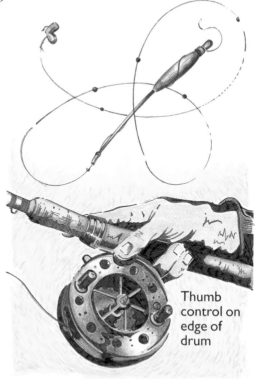

Thumb control on edge of drum

grease. You can't trot effectively with sinking line, and at distance or in a quickish current it's hopeless to try. The float will be pulled all over the place and you'll be able to do very little about it.

The angler is applying side strain to a barbel intent on using the current to win sanctuary in dense reedbeds.

There's a great temptation to use as light a float as possible, but, provided it is well shotted, the float's size does not really matter. A big float is easier to control and see – both vital considerations. In fact, if the sunlight is a problem, consider using Polaroid glasses and/or an eyeshade. Sometimes a hat with a wide brim will be enough. Trotting on a windy day is even more difficult and calls for a float that you can see to the limit of the range over which you are fishing.

'Holding back' is one of the most important skills in trotting. It's simple really: every now and again you just slow the float down so that the bait rises off the bottom to a lesser or greater degree. This tactic provokes what, in trout fishing, is accurately called an 'induced take', and it's just the same situation when a roach, chub or barbel is confronted by, say, a worm or a maggot. It's that little rise that triggers off the instant feeding response. Don't overdo this trick – it can misfire by whisking the bait away from under the fishes' noses – but always try to make sure the float is moving through the swim a little more slowly than the current itself, as this often proves irresistible.

One of the greatest skills in trotting is mending the line. This means lifting it off the water every time it forms a bow and laying it down straight behind the float again. If you don't mend the line the float will be pulled off course and striking will be very difficult because of that disastrous loop! The longer the rod the greater its ability to lift and mend, and this is why a long rod is essential for trotting.

even bring them up-river towards you. You might find, for example, that you start by catching at forty yards but by the end of the session you've got fish almost under your rod tip. Barbel, in particular, will sometimes even nose around between your legs.

What if you are sure that the fish are there but you're not catching them? Well, perhaps the bait is going too fast through the shoal – often a problem with barbel. If it is barbel you're after, try slowing down the bait. To do this you may have to push the float up so that the rig is fishing considerably over depth. If the float is big enough it should drag the bait behind it without giving too many false bites. If you're getting these, increase the size of the float, and never worry about doing this. Also, try holding the float back altogether. To do so you might have to keep the rod tip high and the line straight to the tip of the float, but it should be easy enough, especially if you've got enough weight down near the hook. Bites, when they come to this technique, are savage in the extreme.

The essence of trotting is working the river and making sure that your bait is presented as naturally as the free offerings trundling alongside it. Perhaps you're mending the line, perhaps you're thinking of a better shotting pattern, perhaps you're wondering how to get the bait as close to an overhanging raft as possible – but the constant factor is that you're always thinking, trying to improve your catch rate. And all the while you're thinking, you're bound to be learning. As your experience grows you'll get an ever clearer idea of how fish are behaving.

Effective and enjoyable as legering is, it seldom explains as much as trotting about what is going on in that mysterious domain beneath the surface. In short, if you keep working at it this lovely style of fishing will put you in tune with the river and the fish every time.

Far left: Phil controls his float perfectly –
rod held high, keeping line off the water
where the currents might drag the float off
course. Float fishing like this is hard but
rewarding work.

Left: Note that rod constantly in action,
the centrepin whirling.

Below: Phil makes his own floats out of
balsa-wood because this allows him to
design individual floats to suit specific
swims. I'm not suggesting that everyone
should do this but it's a good idea to
take a wide selection of floats with you for
each session.

A handsome chub
and the home-
made float that
helped to catch it.

Nightfall Barbel

With the arrival of the autumn floods and frosts, the days of long-trotting and wading are virtually over. As the sun sinks from view, an owl works a field across the river, while the badgers shuffle through the wood, yawning after long hours in their sett. The daylight world is closing down but another, more secretive one is opening up – and that's what's happening in the barbel swims too.

It's widely accepted that barbel feed nocturnally at any time of the year. In the autumn, however, night becomes their preferred time – although I would not say the

Left: The sun sets over an autumn river – exactly the time when fish will really be on the prowl.

Below: Twilight is an excellent time of day to try for autumn barbel, as this superb fish shows.

same about the other seasons. Perhaps the darkness gives them a blanket of security which is necessary to them as river temperatures fall. For we are talking about hard, cold days of erratic water levels, when the steady patterns of the summer river have been harshly interrupted and the barbel need some encouragement to feed. Night gives them that incentive.

It's always hazardous to try to predict or interpret any species' precise reactions to a given situation, but at least if you keep asking questions you may come up with a few answers that boost that all-important quality of confidence.

One thing that is certain is that barbel now begin to move around towards twilight – a period of real wakening for the species. This is particularly so in October and November, which for the barbel angler are among the best months of the year. The key is to choose the right swim. You won't be wandering and watching at night, when the autumn wind has a chill, so you must be quite confident of your choice of pitch.

Often the ideal nightfall barbel swim will be close to a prolific summer one, although it will probably be a little deeper. If the ideal summer depth is 4–5ft, in the autumn you might be looking for a patch of 6–7ft, and if it is under the shelter of trees, all the better. The Master Angler knows the benefit of a tree canopy to barbel: by enhancing the darkness that little bit more it adds to their sense of security.

The swim will probably be a stretch where the water runs just a little more slowly than the average for the river. I'm not talking about dead water here – it's simply that the water just out from the swim flows perhaps half a mile per hour faster. This may be a small difference but it's a subtly important one to barbel. Look out too for an area which will offer shelter in times of flood – here again trees figure strongly, as does any indentation in the bank. Shelter isn't vital

Summer swims can often fish well right into autumn. This particular spot was only about 4ft deep but still held a good number of fish.

Split cane and a centrepin reel – it could be a shot from the fifties!

yet, as the floods aren't roaring through, but the barbel know they can't be far off.

Begin to bait up carefully from around mid-afternoon. Don't overdo it, because you can't be sure how many barbel you'll be expecting once night falls, but keep putting in a steady stream. What bait you choose depends on your reading of the swim. For example, if it's carpeted with gudgeon or small dace – both of which will probably move out when the barbel move in – they will make big inroads into maggots or casters. Or if there are still lots of eels about, anything meaty is hardly the perfect night-time bait. In either situation you might try corn – dyed and flavoured if necessary – along with a mix of mashed bread. Some anglers prefer boiled baits, special pastes or chopped luncheon meat or Peperami. As well as being too large for minnows to get their lips round, these all give out a constant stream of odour.

Should you use a swimfeeder or a straight lead? Well, a straight lead may be the better bet if you are using larger baits and you are sure that you have already laid down an effective carpet of food. After all, a straight lead will register bites better and you will run much less risk of spooking fish on the retrieve or even the cast. Also, bites are more easily hit. If you're using maggots and casters you'll probably want to stick with the feeder, but don't be slavish about its use: it's all too easy to put one on and rely on it willy-nilly. Always ask yourself: do I really need a feeder here?

Now that you're all set up there is one last consideration. As far as bite detection is concerned, once darkness has set in there is no better technique than touch legering (see pages 44–5). Master it and you will never regret the hours spent.

Butt Indicators

Now that nearly all anglers use quivertips for bite indication with a legered bait, the butt indicator is almost forgotten on moving water. In the past we simply pinched bread onto the line between the reel and the first eye of the rod. The stronger the current the bigger the piece of bread. The rod would be pointed towards the bait as accurately as possible and the bread bobbin would hang about 1ft beneath the butt. While you couldn't use the set-up in fast water, it was ideal for slower stretches, bends and eddies.

Nowadays clip-on bobbins are widely available and for night fishing you can insert an isotope, so there is no need even to train a torch on the bobbin. If the current is a little fast for the standard bobbin, simply clip on one or two large shot until it is counterbalanced against the pull of the water.

So what are the advantages of a butt indicator over a quivertip? Quivertips are effective and rightly popular, but the butt indicator offers one or two extra benefits.

Above all, it offers just a little less resistance to a shyly feeding fish, and this gives you more time to strike and the fish more time to mouth the bait with a feeling of security. This is vital with big, cautious

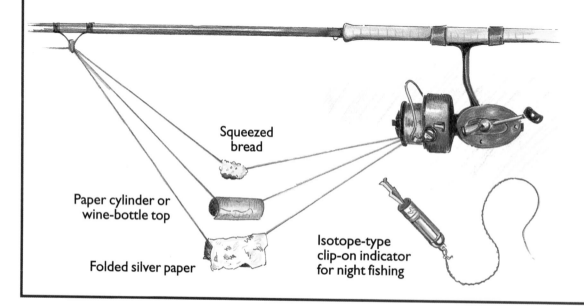

Squeezed bread

Paper cylinder or wine-bottle top

Folded silver paper

Isotope-type clip-on indicator for night fishing

These anglers have crowded together – yet the fish are 800 yards away!

Fishing the Floods

roach or even chub in autumn and winter, when bites are very wary.

Often the bobbin will simply twitch once or twice and then a few seconds later rise steadily to the butt. You rarely miss with the strike, which can't be said of the quivertip. There are times, especially when you are fishing a little upstream, when the bobbin will twitch and then drop towards the ground. Again the strike is almost always met with the thump of a well-hooked fish.

Like any method of indication, you will get false bites from passing weed and rubbish. These you will soon learn to recognize and ignore, as you wait for a real fish to come along.

Before the floods of late autumn begin, it's a good idea to earmark swims that will come into play when the water rises and colours. Take an hour or two to walk along your favourite stretches, imagining what they'll be like once the water is up. While the river is still low, make a note of what these swims are like and if there are any snags that could cause problems later. Look at the bottom make-up, at the contours, and note anything that might prove useful later on, when you're fishing totally blind.

What sort of areas should you look for? Certainly, deeper holes close to the bank are well worth investigating. They are not dead holes, these poky little bays full of silt and washed-up branches, but the current moves more slowly through them and they always look enticing. If there are trees brushing in the water, all the better, because these will slow down the flood as it pours through the swim. At average levels, these areas will be full of eddies, possibly with a bit of gentle slack water as well. The insides of bends are also well worth looking at.

Gradually build up a mental map of what the river will be like when the water is up and pushing, and work out all those places that will offer fish some shelter but will still have some flow. Remember: fish don't like still, dirty water.

Aim to fish somewhere close in to the bank, because the greater the distance between you and the bait, the more rubbish will festoon your line. Also, the further you have to cast, the more pressure the water will exert on the line and the greater the chance of the bait being pulled out of a killing area. In short, you're looking for a tight, close-in area where, because you are almost on top of your fish, you can present a bait very accurately.

Let's imagine it's been raining for three or four days and now, come the weekend, the

A perfect flood-time swim sandwiched between fallen trees. There's also a good flow through it, which should keep the bottom relatively clean.

river is really on the march. First of all you'll be thinking about your bait; its colour, size and smell are the three key considerations. Breadflake works exceptionally well in such situations – the white seems to glow in even the most chocolate-coloured water. You can flavour it with cheese essence or anything you think will draw the fish. Luncheon meat is another proven winner in flood times. The one thing to avoid at times like this is maggot on a size 18 hook. You could sit there for hours waiting for a bite while the man next door legering a great lump of sausage is catching chub after chub.

When it comes to method, above all concentrate on keeping as little line in the water as you can. You might try using a float if you can trundle this around the area

Swims like this are ideal and you can tackle them from close up. Almost all the surrounding trees will prove a bonus in providing cover.

without it snagging or being pulled under by the force of the water. A great deal depends on the savagery of your swim, but if it is float-fishable, then try that – you will find lots of advantages to it. You can set the float so that it's almost laying-on, way over depth and just pulling slowly around the swim. The float will tend to sit up and then shoot under when you get a bite – all very exciting.

However, sometimes during a flood you really need to keep the bait still. The fish seem to need time to home in on the smell the bait is giving out and if it's constantly on the move then they will become confused and not be able to find it. At times like this you still need to keep as much line out of the water as possible, so for once it's best not to touch leger because this involves keeping a lot of line under the surface. Instead, with the rod up high, use a quivertip or even just watch the top itself if the rod is not too stiff. Whatever you do, don't use a quivertip that

A swim like this will be fishable even when the river is 5ft above its usual level and raging through.

Chub will fall under any sort of conditions. Their eyes are big and their sense of smell is acute, but make sure you use a big, attractive bait.

A stunning chub taken from a high, swollen river. The angler had built up his swim over a couple of hours, tempting the fish to feed.

is constantly bent right round because it's not up to the job. And don't assume that during a flood takes will be steam-train affairs – even a big chub picking up a big bait in a big flood can give a very sensitive knock, so bite indication still needs to be delicate and you must concentrate hard.

Canopied by trees, and fishing a tight little swim as the river howls past, you really feel in touch with the fish. It's almost as though you can sense them breathing on the line. And yet if you're not catching them you must rack your brains for a slight improvement that will make all the difference. For example, try lifting the bait 2–3in off the bottom every now and again, helping to induce a take from a half-hungry fish. Or try taking all the shot or lead off the line for a cast or two, and let a big bait just swirl around naturally in the eddies. This may well pay off, because not all the fish will be right down on the bottom, and chub in particular will cruise near the surface in any type of water.

Move to the Mills

As the autumn advances and winter looms, fish migrate in substantial numbers along rivers both big and small. Roach in particular begin to move toward the mills, both to the upstream, ponded areas and also into the mill pools themselves. But why mills should prove such an attraction for roach shoals we can only guess at.

Naturally, the ponded areas are slower and deeper and offer fish more stable water conditions in times of both frost and flood – despite the modern curse of insensitive, inexperienced sluice-gate management, which is the ruination of so many of our rivers. Properly, in normal circumstances, these upstream areas should have a slow flow and the water should be nicely up to bank level – exactly the conditions roach adore when temperatures begin to fall.

With mill pools too, it's easy to see the benefits for roach. Again, they are deeper, an obvious enticement in cold, clear weather, and when the water does rise there are decent slacks always around the central flow of water. Also, spawning will take place in the quicker, shallower water close to the pools when spring arrives, so some roach move up there in anticipation of the spawning act.

The Master Angler is aware that fish weigh their options: the more an area has to offer, the more they will favour it over swims and stretches that are more restrictive. They like to have great flexibility in their living quarters, so that they don't have to move far to find a piece of water that suits them better.

Let's look at fishing the ponded areas. Light legering works well and so does float fishing, but above all, don't be afraid to try either approach right up to the sluices themselves, where the water begins to speed

Left: Ponded areas always look so serene and that is why they attract big fish. The reedbeds and overhanging trees here are a further attraction.

Below: Autumn sunlight streams over the mill as we look upstream onto the ponded area – always a magnet for big roach at this time of year.

In late autumn the ponded areas hold roach and bream in plenty. You will also find that the bigger chub begin to move into stretches like this and can be caught if the groundbaiting is really thoughtful.

Below: Millpools are always attractive places but particularly in autumn, when the fish move up into them looking for warmth and a variety of currents and depths.

Right: Churches and roach swims often seem to go together, which is possibly because historically churches and mills were often built in the same sort of area on the river.

up before disappearing through the mill. Sometimes fish can be packed into even the most unlikely places.

Also, be mobile, because the roach shoals will. Just because you've left a group in one particular place at night, don't expect them to be there the next morning. Roach move up and down the quarter of a mile or so upstream of the mill and they could be anywhere along it. So, if you're not getting bites, simply move until you begin to find fish. And keep your eyes open, for like you, pike know that roach are heavily concentrated at this time of year, and it's very common to see them attack on this type of stretch.

It can pay to leger and float-fish at the same time until you hit a shoal. Put a light leger rod out with a quivertip so that you can see it quite clearly. This covers one area, and then if you trot here and there you are

Above: Notice how the shallows on this river have been cleaned of silt – probably by swans. But that won't stop the roach coming in to feed during the evening.

Below: Cattle also clear the bottom of silt and silkweed and therefore provide enticing tabletops for feeding roach.

Above: A slash of gravel exposed initially by waterfowl but kept clean by roach.

Below: An emptying pool clears the bottom of rubbish, attracting feeding fish.

saturating the stretch of river in front of you. Since there are days when roach prefer moving bait to a stationary one, you are covering all options. It's hard work and it's not restful but it catches fish.

In either the pools or the ponded areas keep a very close eye for clean gravel areas, often found where the water shallows to some extent. After dark, it doesn't matter how shallow these places are – the roach will still come in there to feed. Often the gravel has been cleared by swans, ducks or wading cattle, but the roach will move in afterwards and make sure that silt and weed don't recolonize the spot.

As for why roach find bare sand and gravel so attractive, some roach experts maintain that they hate feeding over any type of noxious bottom. And who can blame them! My own observations suggest that it's probably because these areas are more fertile and food can be found more easily.

Autumn Stillwaters

Stalking Carp

Carp stalking on lakes is one of angling's most demanding challenges, and in return provides some of the best excitement. You take in all the water has to offer, begin to see everything it is doing and learn to interpret the tiniest signs of fish and activity.

Carp can be easy to spot, but often even the biggest fish are not. I remember many occasions when big carp were present in clear, shallow water and yet they were all but invisible. It's fantastic, and nobody really knows how they do it.

So how does the would-be Master Angler set about the problem of elusive autumn carp? First of all it's a question of patiently sitting and watching, rather than rushing to

Left: When you are stalking carp, dress drably and move very, very slowly. Scan the water every time you take a yard's pace.

Above right: A perfect area to stalk carp in: the wind has pushed into this bay, building up scum which itself harbours all sorts of foodstuffs. The carp will move in here for both warmth and food.

start fishing. Provided it's a quiet water, you can sit for hours without being disturbed and, more importantly, without the fish being becoming alarmed. Generally, the pinnacle of stalking carp is reached on smaller waters, because everything is more intimate and intense – so much so that sometimes you really think you can hear the fish breathing.

Let's suppose you've found an area of water which is undisturbed and is, in all probability, hemmed in by fallen trees and branches – just the sort of place shunned by most carp anglers, with their space-hungry equipment. However, the carp, though there, are not making any obvious statement. What do you see? There may be one or two large bubbles that rise and explode on the surface: they can be oily affairs, looking for all the world as though the bottom is just releasing gas. Possibly that's all it is, but you can't be

sure and, more often than not, a slowly moving carp is the culprit. But bubbles come in all shapes and forms. For example, sometimes you might just spy a patch of small bubbles fizzing before quickly dying out – a dead give-away.

Often there's just a suspicion of clouded water: not a great smoke-screen of silt being churned up, but just a stain on the water – something you've got to look at over and over before you're at all sure about it. In fact, you're probably only convinced that it was caused by fish when it dies away and you notice it by its absence.

See that dying lily stem twitch? Did you notice that broken branch shudder and give out little rings? Why do you think that little fish skipped clear of the water then – just for the fun of it? Did you notice that slight welling – an easy, gentle rippling effect – in that pocket of dead-calm water? And did you

mark down the patch of flat water in the middle of that ripple? All these clues and many more are there for you to pursue in the confidence that carp are present.

One of the attractions of stalking is that it allows you to adopt the widest possible variety of techniques. You can use surface baits, you can float-fish or you can freeline. Natural baits all work well, but so do pastes and boilies. Again, it's up to you.

You will have noticed how often I've stressed the need to think hard and make your own decisions – that's because each situation is different. Do what you think is right in each case and don't worry about breaking rules that are not applicable anyway. Many carp anglers are realizing that the unexpected frequently pays off and that stereotyped fishing brings mediocre and predictable results.

As for tackle, you don't really need anything special, even though purpose-made stalking rods are now on the market. Concentrate on the details – for a start, a wide variety of floats of all sizes, colours and shapes. Make sure you have a good selection of hooks to suit each type of bait. Take split shot with you and perhaps line putty. A pot of bogey can also be excellent if you're going to use particles – for example, hempseed or casters (see pages 76–7).

Probably my favourite baits for stalking are all naturals of one sort or another and in that definition I include maggots, because although they are a particle bait they are also a living thing. There is something fitting about presenting a natural bait to a carp that you can see actually feeding in the bottom silt. What could be more natural than a lobworm, a bunch of brandlings, a couple of redworms, a knot of wriggling maggots, a slug, a couple of leeches, two or three caddis grubs, or even something totally bizarre like a small dead elver?

Opposite left: A good carp moving under some trees. However, it has bolted because it has seen the float cocked in the water. Even though this float is a transparent one, the fish is well aware of its presence.

Above: Here the float is laid flat on the water with nothing protruding beneath the surface. This carp is not afraid and obviously sees it as just a piece of wood.

Right: This fine fish was the fitting reward for dedicated stalking, one of the most versatile and productive approaches for carp.

Playing a good carp in the bay of a large water – a crucial time after after all the waiting.

A lovely autumnal common carp held for the setting sun.

The same type of approach can even be tried on the surface. There are times when carp do wise up to traditional floating baits but if you see them browsing in those areas where a scum has built up during the day, you will see that surface feeding is very much on their minds. The earlier part of autumn often sees great hatches of large moths and beetles, many of which come to grief in the water, to be washed up against the windward bank. Carp know this and profit from it and so can the thinking angler. It was Chris Yates, I think, who first advocated artificial moths for carp at this time of the year in this sort of water, but a couple of expired natural ones probably do at least as well and are much easier to tie! The only problem with them is that distance casting is impossible.

But once again there are no rules, and it's simply up to the thinking angler to work out his own method of attack. Nothing you do can be wrong unless you're not catching a fish. Apart from one thing, that is: never go into a snag-ridden area with line that you know is too light to cope with the situation. It's a crime to fish for carp which you know you have little chance of landing.

One last tip, if the fish are there and feeding and you're not getting bites, think carefully about the position of your line. This is something carp can be very aware of and if they see it in mid-water then often they will shy away. It's at times like this that it pays to lay the line hard along the bottom for at least 3–4ft away from the hook. So, if you're using a float, set it massively over depth, or if legering, make use of a back-lead – small things make all the difference.

Above: The majesty of an autumn carp – this fish is only small but look how the colours are already beginning to glow at this time of year.

Below: The stalking carp angler will derive as much benefit as possible from screening features like boathouses and overhanging trees.

Bream Days

Often the warmer autumn days see the very best of the season's bream fishing, especially on large lakes, pits and reservoirs. One of the reasons for this is the decline in natural food stocks and the fishes' growing desire to feed up hard before the frosts come. But also, as water temperatures begin to teeter then fall, the bream seem to move together into large shoals, in which they will remain throughout the winter. Whereas in the summer it's very common to see them moving in smaller groups, with the onset of cold weather their behaviour changes noticeably.

As a result, it's not unusual to see twenty anglers sitting around the water and only one catching, despite what I said above about the

You will often find anglers huddled together on one bank even though there is little sign of fish or feeding activity. This tends to be a herd reaction – it's far better to figure out things for yourself.

quality of autumn bream sport. The fact is that usually most of them are simply fishing away from the bream shoals and any chance of success depends on the fish drifting into their swim. The problem is that at this time of year the shoals are often moving slowly, if at all, and are often panicked by the activities of groups of anglers, including the splash of feeders all around them. It's not an easy time to fish – especially when the weather is mild and calm and the water is dead still.

I don't doubt that most anglers have a preconceived idea of which swim they're going to fish before they even arrive at the water. At best, they will choose the one that looks the most comfortable in the prevailing wind conditions. What nine out of ten anglers never do is actually scout the water hard before settling on a particular pitch. Again and again on my local lake, just half a mile away from my home, I see fishermen drawing a blank all day long yet there will be bream moving in great masses only fifty or at

I love this photograph of an elderly angler with his binoculars scanning the water. Significantly, he went on to move to another position and was the only man to catch fish that particular day.

most 100 yards away. It's as though these anglers, patient as they are, remain absolutely blind to what the water is telling them. They've probably never even thought about another approach, but – and I don't mean this unkindly – such ignorance is costing them dearly session after session.

So, look long and hard, because even on the largest lake, and even in wind, there will be clues. If the surface is still, and the water is not deep, then the true fish watcher will nearly always know exactly where bream are to be found. Naturally on deeper pits this is more difficult, but even there the odd fish will be seen rolling.

Binoculars are an advantage because they make the most of the tip of a fin, a patch of flat water or a sheet of popping bubbles. Look for the odd black back breaking out of the ripple. Keep your eyes open for any bow-waves – especially in the morning or evening.

Look out too for bream coming half out of the water. You will see clearly their heads and backs – sure signs of fish on the move, and usually willing to feed.

A lot is said about bream patrol routes: those age-old trails around a water that the fish habitually follow. They do indeed use them, especially in summer. But in the autumn bream will often remain in quite a tight area for up to two or three days or even more, and sometimes until they are pushed out by angling pressure or natural causes. Often these fish will move barely at all, especially if there's a natural food source to be exhausted. Patrol routes play no part here, so you shouldn't assume that sooner or later everyone around the lake will get a fish.

As well as fish watching, ask the bailiff about any significant bream catches in the recent past. If fish have been caught from one spot one day, then they may well be in that same area the next. Local knowledge can prove invaluable.

If you arrive at the water and no one has caught anything at all, then fish a different bank or along a different line. Or why not fish along several different lines? Cast in various directions, leaving the bait three or four minutes until fish are located. It doesn't have to be a proper bite: line bites will give them away just as efficiently. A cast of two or three minutes is probably quite enough to prove whether bream are lying along that line or not.

Even if you are settled in a swim, trying to build up one particular area, cast a second line at different angles if you are not locating bream. Unless you're actually catching fish on the first rod, use it to keep searching the water in front of you.

Like barbel anglers, nearly all bream men attack with the swimfeeder, and this, in the right hands at the right time and in the right place, can be a killing method. But it's not a

This photograph was taken as the sun was low and it shows a feeder hitting the surface. Notice the splash and the slashing action of the line as it enters the water. Bream are very sensitive and cannot help but pick up disturbances like this.

method that should be used exclusively or without thought. Picture those calm, sunlit days when the water really does rock to the splash of a feeder. Bream are frequently old and inevitably wise fish, so can you think of a bigger give-away to the angler's presence and the ambush he's planning? In conditions like this, try catapulting bait into the area, scattering tiny little balls of it around like rain, and then use a straight lead, such as a fixed paternoster, as this causes much less disturbance.

As for bait, it pays to take the greatest possible care of it. Too many anglers attack bream with old and tired baits, unaware that they can be unbelievably fussy. Maggots are fine but make sure they're excellent ones and try them in cocktails with casters or small redworms or a tip of sweetcorn. Try the odd surprise – for example, corn on a size 8 hook with a good wad of flake. Very often a fish will take this even on the drop. A full lobworm can be very effective: while most bream anglers favour smaller, apparently

*Left: An autumn bream
comes to the net at sunset.*

*Below: It rolls, nearly beaten. But notice the
swimfeeder – is this always necessary?*

*Right: The fish is
played out at last …*

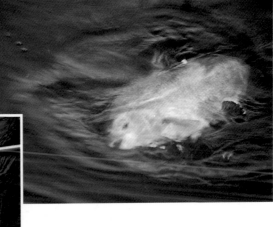

… and it's safely in the net.

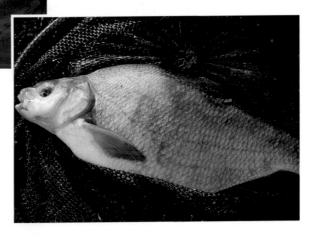

*A lovely bream, just beginning
to build up winter depth.*

more attractive baits, don't neglect the large, old-fashioned ones.

With careful observation – understanding both the fish and the water – you can minimize dramatically the long hours of waiting, and increase your enjoyment. Then, when you start taking bream, you will know why you're catching them and be able to apply the same knowledge the next time. Applying this insight, rather than sitting for hours hoping for the best, is part of the Master Angler's stock in trade.

The Paternoster Rig

One of the most finicky feeders among our freshwater species, a good-sized bream will take a bait very gently between its lips and perhaps move off a foot or so, gradually moving the bait deeper into its mouth. If it feels any resistance at all, the bait will be rejected or pulled from the lips as the fish's hold is very delicate.

It's this type of feeding behaviour that makes the presentation of a legered bait absolutely essential. So, if you are going to use a sliding link-leger you must be extremely careful that the line actually moves through the link. If it doesn't, the lead will bounce along the bottom after the fish and the bait will almost certainly be dropped. Strike after strike will be missed. The two ways to set up the sliding link efficiently are to use a reasonably heavy bomb – at least 1oz – and a low-resistance ring at the end of the link. These two additions will ensure that the line at least moves to a reasonable extent.

However, the majority of successful bream anglers see the fixed paternoster as the most efficient way to turn those pick-ups into proper strikable bites. The diagram shows the essentials of the fixed paternoster. It's a very simple rig whose great advantage is that it allows the bream to pick up the bait and wander for those vital few seconds without feeling any resistance at all. By the time the bomb is felt the bait is deep in the fish's mouth and past the point of easy ejection. Striking the bites is simplicity itself and in fact you can almost sit on your hands and wait for the reel handle to move round.

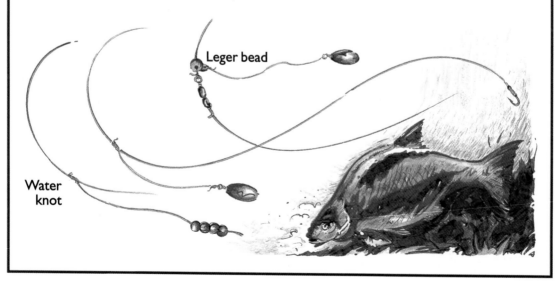

Leger bead

Water
knot

Perch Bliss

How do you tell if the predators striking into a shoal of small fleeing roach are perch or pike? It can be hard to decide, but there are some useful pointers.

Frequently, unlike a pike, a perch will pursue a single fish for several yards, snapping at it, worrying at its tail, slowing it down before closing in for the kill. Also, perch will often hunt in a group, so there will be attacks here and there on the surface, whereas the pike hunts alone, lunging at its prey. If you're particularly lucky you'll see the erect, menacing dorsal fins of perch clearing the surface as they skim about, mouths agape, the hunting frenzy on them.

In the autumn many waters are beginning to lose their algal blooms and clearing considerably – perfect conditions for perch,

Perch flashing into a shoal of small fry. Notice the four or five attack points. These indicate the presence of a shoal of preyfish.

which hunt predominantly by eyesight. And by now there will be vast shoals of roach, bream and even carp fry reaching a perfect size for perch fodder. Of course, the perch is a voracious feeder all year round, but the autumn is a bonanza for them, and you might just as well take advantage of this fact.

In any water perch numbers can be very variable: nobody really stocks them and their breeding patterns are notoriously unpredictable. In fact, even a large stillwater may have only one or two shoals of big fish, so location will often prove critical. And for this you can't beat visual sightings: once you see perch hunting, then a bait placed right in the killing zone stands an excellent chance of being taken.

But you can't always rely on visual location, and there are times when the water seems dead. This is the time to tie on a lure: a small plug cast here and there might not actually take the fish but you can often get a follow or feel a pluck or two, and then follow up with a bait.

Left: The perch angler's boat awaits. If you can get a boat on any water and you are confident about using it, then do seize the opportunity. Since locating fish is all-important, so is mobility.

Right: A stunning autumn perch. Take great care to avoid injury from the dorsal fin.

Right: Perch striking their prey. This is where a drift float comes in or, if you've got one, a small boat.

If this approach doesn't work, then try a cut-down, modified drift float of the sort that pike fishermen use. With the wind behind you, you can get a suitable bait out 100 yards or more and really explore the water, looking for any shoals of big perch that might be holed up way beyond normal casting range.

Failing this, remember that perch like to hang around snags – all fish do, but with perch it's an obsession. In fact, if you simply anchor a boat for a while, they will congregate round the rope and underneath the hull. So, look for fallen trees, lily beds, boathouses, landing-stages, or any structure that they might find comforting.

Probably the best all-round perch bait is a small live fish, 2–4in in length. Gudgeon have always had a good press but small roach and rudd are also excellent. Baby perch work very well too, but pay no heed to that old nonsense that says you should cut off the spiky dorsal fin!

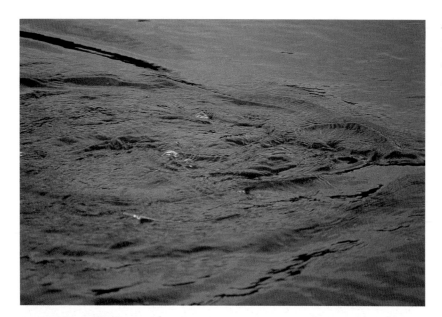

A perch boils under the float – a much better method of bite indication than legering.

A typical shot of a beaten big perch coming towards the net with the deadbait, typically taken head first, still protruding from its mouth.

Nevertheless, my own preference for really big perch is a fresh dead fish. I believe that big perch don't like to hunt anything frisky but much prefer to slide up to an immobile but juicy meal and simply sip it in. Certainly my own three biggest perch have come this way.

Lobworms were traditionally one of the great perch baits, but they gradually fell from favour and now we've forgotten how to fish them for perch. You need a lot – not just enough for the hook baits. And then about

half an hour must be spent chopping the lobs into ½ in segments and throwing these raw into the swim. This is not nice work and I don't blame you if you don't want anything to do with it, but it's the blood and the squirming segments that get the perch interested and then feeding. After that, a lobworm with a hook buried in it will be taken with gusto.

Maggots also catch perch, but then many anglers use them and that boosts the success rate. There's an interesting point to bear in mind here. Many's the time that a pleasure angler or even a matchman has been catching small roach and things have gone quiet, only for the next bite to come from a 1½lb perch. It's easy to see what has happened: the constant groundbaiting has brought in a roach shoal and the activity has focused the attention of perch, which, after a while, have moved in to feed. In a situation like this even a couple of maggots on a size 16 are scoffed as the perch move through.

Of course, to the Master Angler this suggests another possibility for location: why

not try to build up a swim, like a matchman would, with groundbait and maggots? Get the small fish going – it's all the better if these happen to be little perch – and most likely the big perch will begin to move in at some point during the day. Have a small livebait working on the fringe of the feeding area with a lobworm or a deadbait in the middle of all the activity. Ring the changes, and keep alert.

And remember the reward: a big perch taken on a sunny autumn afternoon is one of freshwater angling's most stirring sights.

This beautiful 3lb perch took a 4in deadbait resting on the bottom, float-fished near fallen branches.

Hooked-up on Perch

Whether you're using deadbaits or livebaits for perch – both are, without doubt, the most killing attractors for big fish – then you are almost certain to run into problems when it comes to hooking. Many an angler has almost cried with frustration after missing run after run from decent fish.

First of all, wherever possible use a float as an indicator. A loafer-style float, for example, gives a precise idea of how long the bite has been in progress and how it is developing. If you can see a float you're more in tune with what a perch is doing.

Make sure that the hook is around the head of the bait: a perch may well attack from behind but once the bait fish is savaged and slowed down it will almost certainly be engulfed head first – the obvious place to put your hook.

Large single hooks are excellent for most perch work, but when there are persistent hooking problems I prefer a double, although in some cases it might have to be a small treble. Experiment to see what you need.

Always strike early: it's much better to miss a fish than have to delve into a deep-hooked one – a situation that generally means bleeding and death and, hopefully, a great deal of remorse on your part. In any case, remember that a missed bite often indicates a smaller fish – not something to eat your heart out about.

Once you've hooked your perch, maintain steady, unrelenting pressure and get the fish in the landing net as soon as you possibly can. For one reason or another, even big perch are usually only lightly hooked and as they approach the net you can expect a lot of head shaking to go on – exactly the time when you are most likely to see that little gudgeon hurled skywards with your hook still attached to it.

Hooking perch is a challenge, so think out your approach and experiment as much as you need to until you get it right – but never forget that the next time will almost certainly be different!

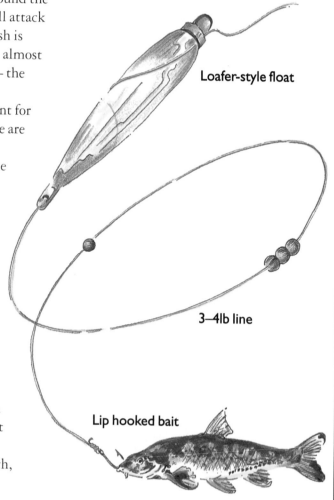

Loafer-style float

3–4lb line

Lip hooked bait

Puddles of Gold

With its stumpy little form, like a golden soup plate, and its small fins, the crucian looks like the joker of the carp pack, but in fact it's a true delight. For a start, it's an absolute Houdini of a fish: I can think of water after water where hardly an angler knows that a crucian is present even when they are there in appreciable numbers. Such concealment is a real skill, and one that few other species have mastered.

But then, even when crucians are known to be present, they can still be the most difficult fish to catch, bar none – and I'm not exaggerating. Of course, there are lakes where they fight fair and square and the float will trundle along and disappear and you could think that you were fishing for roach or rudd that had never seen an angler before. But I know of only about two waters in the world where this continues to happen, and I put it down to the crucians there being of intellectually sub-standard stock!

As for the rest of the species, you are facing a real challenge. However, the challenge isn't quite as great if you have worked out how the crucian thinks and behaves. Once you've taken all their bizarre little characteristics into account, you'll start catching them.

Crucians like this are worth any amount of trial and tribulation.

Let's look first of all at their annoying habit of sucking and blowing food. Although I've no idea why they do this, I have no doubt that it's a common crucian practice. They take a food item into their mouths, hold it two or three seconds and then blow it out, repeating the process up to twenty or even thirty times. What I'm convinced is happening is that they are softening the bait up ready to chew and swallow. I say this because the number of times this process is repeated seems to depend on the toughness of the food item. For example, a lively tadpole will be sucked in and out perhaps twenty-five times before being swallowed, whereas a piece of soft bread might receive the treatment only four or five times. And a tail of lobworm could well be dizzy before it finally goes down the throat for the last time!

The obvious approach suggested by this habit is to go for baits that are as soft as possible but still allow you to cast them and stay on the hook. Wasp grubs, certainly young, fresh ones, I have often found excellent. They just hang there all limp and squashy, and seem to attract very positive bites from crucians, although not everyone can lay their hands on wasp grubs, of course.

The next best bait that I have found is a really soft paste made out of the groundbait in use. Do make sure it is firm enough to hang from the hook for an under-hand cast and keep reasonably intact on the bottom for ten or fifteen minutes. If it dissolves round the hook into a molehill, that doesn't matter much because the crucian will come along and suck it and the hook into its mouth in the same instant. Believe me, the soft bait approach really works and it's worth trying to come up with your own ideas on this.

A rare shot of a crucian carp sipping bread from the surface – proof if you want it that crucians are not always bottom feeders.

Heron-like patience is often required for crucians. Notice the reedbeds and the lilies in front, all providing screening and attractive snags for fish.

Left: Into a crucian at last. Never rush the fish, even if it is clearly small – the hook may not be well set.

Below: The exhausted crucian lies beaten on the lilies.

Your presentation will have to be precise with a fish that bites so delicately, and hardly ever roars off with the bait like other members of the carp family. For this reason alone, a float is almost always an essential item with crucians. I have, on rare occasions, caught them on leger tackle, but am convinced that it's best to use a float. However, it must be set up to register the slightest movement, for if the crucian is simply sucking and blowing and not moving, the float may only dip ¼in at most. And even that may be considered a bold bite. Therefore I don't like to use any laying-on techniques at all: I like to plumb the depth of the swim exactly and present the bait just on

Hemp, sweetcorn and bread – you rarely need any other baits than these for crucians.

the bottom. This can be a problem in a wind if the float begins to move around, but you'll just have to move a back-stop up the line and use a wind-cheater-style float. This should work well, especially at close range.

Never worry, as some anglers do, about fishing at the margins, because here another species characteristic comes into play. Crucians absolutely adore the feel of the bank around them, especially the security of overhanging trees and, most importantly, sunken tree roots. They revel in tree roots, twisting in and out of them, and rubbing their bodies against them. If they can't find tree roots, then reedbeds or lily stems will do. The important thing to bear in mind is that their nature demands this type of cover, most frequently found under the rod tip.

Another little crucian ruse is that on many waters they are quite happy to take floating food at night, provided it is presented hard in to the bank or under an overhanging tree. This all fits with what I've said so far: the crucian carp is a secretive little fellow, hating to show itself to the angler, but, in the dead of night, it may well choose to leave the bottom and feed on the surface.

The crucian carp does not seem to range widely around a water. Occasionally you will see a shoal move from one weedbed to another but by and large this fish can spend all its life – or the vast majority of it anyway – in the shade of one single tree. You will always find a recognizable crucian at home there: perhaps you will catch it or perhaps you will just see it slide back into the shelter of the tree root.

What brings the crucian out? What makes it want to go on a feeding spree. Well, they certainly adore the taste and the smell of hempseed. Hard hempseeds they inevitably suck and blow innumerable times, and in my experience it pays to use crushed and ground hemp in a soft paste or cloud. That way, they get all the scents they crave and can just slurp in nice sloppy items of food.

And the best time of day to catch crucians? Well, obviously at night or at dawn, when the fish think that no angler will be up and about. In fact, when you catch a crucian before sunrise, it comes in with a totally puzzled expression on its face as if saying, 'What the hell are you doing here so early?' You see, crucian carp think that they have us totally worked out. But the Master Angler knows that it pays to be one step ahead.

Rudd on the Surface

If there are rudd in your waters, then you've struck gold, for these are stunningly beautiful fish. You can catch them off the bottom, like other species, and certainly a rudd or two will come along if you are building up a bag of tench or bream. But this is not real rudd fishing.

Traditional rudding on pits means taking fish off the top, and for that you've got to draw them up and keep them there with floating baits. The two ideals are Chum Mixer or similar biscuits, or, better still, casters.

The trick is to sit with the wind at your back, catapulting bait out on a regular basis so that it floats around the lake. Sometimes you can have a trail about 100 yards long before fish begin to show. Of course, there won't always be rudd – or perhaps carp will come up first – but you'll soon know if rudd are present from those distinctive flashes of scarlet or gold.

The trick is simply to get your bait in among the feeding fish with as much precision and as little commotion as possible. A powerful match rod, 3lb main line and a well-filled spool are the basic tools. A long waggler float is next – its length gives stability and copes with the shot that you might need if you are fishing at long range. For the hook length, which should be about 4ft of 2–2½lb line, Double Strength lines are ideal because they give you that extra bit of power with no added diameter. On the hook try one or two casters on a size 14 or 16 or a small cat or dog biscuit on a size 10 or 12.

Cast the float into the fringes of the activity and watch carefully. Once you see it skidding across the surface and dipping under, give a slow, gentle yet powerful strike. The further out you're fishing the further back you will have to stretch the rod before contact is made. Do not snatch at these bites, otherwise a breakage is very likely indeed.

Once rudd are on the surface and located, actually catching them can be quite simple and straightforward, so don't lose heart or patience if it takes a while to get them in your sights. Talking about sights, once you've seen a pristine 2lb rudd glowing in the autumnal light, you'll understand better than ever the wisdom of being a fisherman.

A very good rudd taken at long range on a floating bait – in this case a well-soaked dog biscuit.

Winter

Footsteps in the frost along the river bank at sunrise … A red-tipped float slipping under the steely water in the gloom of a roach fisher's evening … A pike swirling in the middle of a bay so violently that the reed stems bend to the ripple and a second later the line peels off the spool … Seeking out chub under the alders when the ice clings to the branches in silver droplets … Dace fishing in dancing shallows that are steaming in the morning sun … Geese honking in towards the water at dusk as the winter carp finally makes its move.

In the dark, cold months, when you're forced to contend with the elements, it's vital to think of the good things about winter fishing and inspire yourself to get out there and make the most of the most challenging of all the seasons.

No matter how severe the cold, how lashing the rain, the Master Angler still has to keep thinking, keep alert – and that means keeping warm and dry. Having the right winter clothing is crucial, as it's impossible to fish properly if you are miserably cold or wet. However, take care when buying winter gear, because much of what's on the market, even some of the expensive and highly recommended items, is barely up to the job of keeping out driving rain over a ten-hour session. Buy outer garments, in particular, with caution, and buy the best you can afford.

Cold and rain are most likely to affect your head, your hands and your feet. A selection of

A freezing day above a mill. Bites are sure to be very difficult to come by, especially in the hours of daylight, and you're probably best to attack the water late in the afternoon and fish the first two or three hours of darkness.

woolly hats is a good idea, as is a heavy balaclava for those freezing dry days. A waterproof hat should have a chin-strap to stop it flying away in strong wind. But if it isn't too cold even a baseball cap with a deep rim can keep your head warm and keep the rain off Polaroid glasses or out of your eyes.

Every really good angler detests wearing gloves, particularly for energetic mobile fishing, but sometimes you have no choice. In such conditions Neoprene gloves offer the best combination of warmth and flexibility, especially those that allow the top end of the thumb and the first two fingers to be folded back onto strips of Velcro.

But it's your feet that bear the brunt of the weather. When you feel like you're standing on blocks of ice your mind will almost certainly be on going home rather than on the fishing. The only answer is to kit yourself out with the right gear. First, a pair of 'moon boots' with separate linings will help on days when the cold is intense and the temperatures rarely, if at all, rise above freezing. For slightly warmer days when walking is in prospect, get some Derri-boots. A pair of thermal thigh waders will allow you to wade out and trot shallow water without feeling any cold at all. Chest waders may not be essential but if ever you have to get in deep, they are what you will need.

The experienced angler will also take along several pairs of dry socks, some of them thermal, in a polythene bag, and keep a couple of warm, dry fleecy towels in the car.

You won't need reminding to include a vacuum flask of hot drink, but it's amazing how many anglers forget or neglect to equip themselves for winter fishing and then abandon a session because of the cold or wet.

Winter Rivers

— Roach on a Freezing Day —

In winter, river roach will almost certainly still be in the vicinity of the mills, as they have been since the later autumn (see pages 101–5). However, the fishing will have become rather more difficult and as the water temperatures have plummeted then the sport will have slowed right down.

Various things work against us at this time of year. For a start, unless the weather has been mild and wet, the river may well be running crystal-clear and when the sky is a brilliant blue and the sun glares down, every minute behavioural difference between the hook bait and the free offerings around it shows up in glaring contrast. Roach don't

Roach and dead sedges seem to go together.

miss a trick and such water conditions are definitely work in their favour.

We must also remember that the fish have been in the area for weeks or even months, and that means they know the water around them very well and are aware of all the different nuances of the currents. This, too, makes it easy for them to detect any bait that seems to be behaving in an awkward or stilted fashion.

Then there is angling pressure: fish will have been caught or hooked or seen their shoal mates lifted from the water and, as a result, they become increasingly suspicious – at times almost unnaturally so. And when it comes to putting pressure on fish stocks, pike are almost as bad as the anglers. They will have realized by now where their food has gone and many will have crowded in to lurk in the reeds, waiting for an unwary victim to swim by. At this time of year you'll see many predatory strikes, each of which reinforces the twitchy outlook of prey fish.

In these circumstances very often the roach will feed very late indeed, and the colder the weather the later they begin. Ten or even eleven o'clock at night is not too late for them to suddenly, unexpectedly start feeding for an hour or so. But night fishing in winter is cold, teeth-chattering work and only for the hardy few. So instead let's look at those fish that are still catchable in the hours of daylight and, despite what I've said before, some are.

One thing in our favour is that we already know where the fish are, so it's one of those rare times when we can skip location and concentrate on working out a strategy to fool them. Above all, we must fish light. Some twenty years ago I wrote an article recommending 7oz nylon hook lengths that had been imported from Poland or wherever

A big roach caught on the float.

A small but perfect fish taken on a bitingly cold day on a millpool. Often the flow of water spurs roach into activity and then they will feed throughout the day.

and had really excited me because fish that I had thought untakable had at last started to bite. I even managed to land a few! Nowadays I wouldn't advocate anything as barmy as that, but there are lessons to be learnt from the response of that group of fish.

Also, we must scale down. You may get away with using a very small float, especially if the flow has decreased and you make that effort to get closer to your fish without scaring them. A float can really stand out like a sore thumb at this time of year, and the fish will be only too aware of it.

Now we come to that crucial combination of hook length and hook. If you've been using a size 16 or 18, now is perhaps the time to try a 20 or even a 22. Scaling down like this helps greatly, although if you've got a 1¾lb roach on the end it's heart-stopping stuff. But it's the line that's the most important thing because that is what makes the maggot or caster behave in an unnatural way. Nowadays there are the co-polymer lines on the market – Drennan Double Strength is a typical brand and the thickness of this brand's 2lb b.s. line is like that of earlier 1lb lines. It's

Monster Roach

Over the years I've become convinced that the very biggest roach do not behave like the normal run of fish and do not migrate to the usual areas late on in the season. Instead, they tend to keep apart, aloof – hard, old fish that in many cases are not just big, but monsters.

However, these wandering giants can be made to concentrate in specific swims by an intensive baiting campaign. The trick is not to introduce too much bait at any one time – you are not expecting a large head of fish – but simply to keep putting it in very regularly – daily if possible. If you can't get to the river each day, you may be able to recruit the help of a local boy. Remember, consistency of baiting is everything.

In the past my successes have come on big, deep, slow holes where I've put in three to four slices of mashed bread a day. I mix it very lumpy and heavy so that it gets down to the bottom and stays there until eaten. It's important to fish these areas fairly regularly – partly to make sure that chub have not moved in, as they will eat the bait and disturb the odd big roach. If you think there are a lot of chub in the swim it is usually best to move to another.

Don't worry if bites are a very long time coming: it's almost better if you have to wait session after session because at least you know small, unwanted fish are not taking the food. Of course, you might want to scale down the amount you're putting in because you don't want rotting bread around the swim. As always, experiment and be flexible, and with any luck, sooner or later that monster roach you've always dreamed of will be yours.

The frost is thick on the trees and there are now times when fish will begin to move up to shoal around bridge areas, which are often deep and sheltered.

A ponded area can be home to chub and bream as well as roach and it pays to groundbait lightly in one or two areas, in the hope that the fish will move in. Often there will be a deeper central channel in such places as well and this deserves special attention.

advisable to use it only as a hook length – perhaps the last 2-3ft of your rig – but it really can improve bait presentation.

In autumn waters a bait dragging the bottom may have worked well, but not now that the roach have seen a good number of them trundle past. The trouble with a dragging bait is that it picks up muck and weed from the bottom, often within the first few feet of the trot, and so begins to look dirty and unnatural. Instead, try sending the bait down the swim just a couple of inches off the bed – an inch if it's fairly regular and there are few dead branches or other debris sticking up.

Alternatively, try feeding bait in very sparingly but very frequently and moving your hook bait down in mid-water. You could, after a while, entice fish off the bottom and if the sun is right you may begin to see them flash as they intercept maggots on the way down. Often a floating caster will do the trick or a maggot left in a little water so that it soaks some up and makes itself buoyant, to counteract the weight of the hook.

This style of fishing can be a frustrating business. You know full well that there are fish down there, and yet you're unable to get a bite. Even a Master Angler can struggle

until he hits on just the right formula to pull
out a fish or two.

Of course, everything changes once the
weather breaks, the temperatures rise, the
clouds scud over, the rain falls and the river
rises and colours. Fish that seemed
uncatchable one day will sometimes
practically walk up the rod forty-eight hours
later. But whether this brings as much
satisfaction as winkling out a single good fish
on an impossible day is for you to decide.

Chub Tactics

Brassy, bronzed and bold, winter chub are
simply magnificent. At the same time they
are difficult, wary creatures that demand
great respect. The Master Angler knows this
but he's not easily deterred. He's willing to
try one of the tried-and-tested approaches to

*Chub will often look for deep, slow bends sheltered
by trees when the going gets really tough.*

Left: Chub and sweetcorn – even in winter this yellow bait really targets the species, partly because of its visibility but also because of its powerful smell.

Below: Creeping and crawling, climbing and cursing all go with chub fishing. There's no swim here really at all and the angler had to climb down a sheer bank and lean against a tree to work his bait just on the inside of the crease – always a killing area.

catching these fish – with perhaps a trick or two of his own thrown in.

First of all, take a look at the deeper, slower stretches of river, where the swims are hard to reach and the chub will be fewer in number but probably large in average size. But bear in mind that actually locating chub in daylight can be difficult. The task is often easier at dusk or nightfall, simply because the fish in these stretches become mobile once the light fades and then they find your carpet of bait rather than you finding them.

If you prefer to find your fish during the day, certain clues will help you. Look out for a single bush on a treeless bank, as chub are likely to be in the area. Again, a bend, a snag or a slight depression might all harbour a fish or two but, equally, they might not!

Roger Miller wading through shallows to bait up a swim that he knows will hold chub after dark.

All in all, unless you have detailed knowledge of the stretch, it's best to wait until the light is beginning to die and then put out the bait and sit back, reasonably confident that a fish or two will wander past you within the next few hours.

How much bait do you put out? Well, not much, because you are not dealing with shoals of smaller chub here – just a handful of big, picky fish. But you do need a carpet that looks good, is visible and holds the fish. Try some mashed bread with larger lumps left in it and then perhaps two or three handfuls of casters. This way the bread is visible and attracts the fish, and the casters hold them as they burrow around looking for more of these tasty morsels. If you leger a piece of breadflake in that area, it's bound to be seen and will probably be taken.

Terminal gear does not have to be complicated – a simple running leger is

Floodwater Thinking

Between October and March, on any river, but especially big rivers, you will be faced from time to time with floodwater conditions. However, just look at the situation positively and you will be surprised how a flooded or rising river can work to your advantage.

There are only two occasions when floodwater really can spell problems. The first is in the late autumn, when the rising river brings down a mass of unwanted rubbish like dying weed and fallen leaves. Of course, you can still fish and fish will still be feeding, but it can be very frustrating. The second occasion is when the flood is the result of snow-melt and the water temperatures plummet. It's very likely that fish really will go almost totally off the feed in both these situations.

Over the years there has been a lot of debate about whether it's best to fish a flooded river when it's rising, stable or falling. I'm not sure any case is proven, although I used to think that a falling river was the best. To some extent I still do, and certainly the fishes' spirits rise as the levels begin to recede. And yet I've known barbel, in particular, really spark into life as soon as the water has colour and force and begins to move up the bank.

In times of flood it's easy to be put off by what seems like a total lack of visibility. Again, I don't think the fish are nearly as bothered by it as we are and I've caught barbel, chub and roach when I've lost sight of even the most obvious bait after it was a fraction of an inch below the surface. Somehow the fish find the food if you're in the right sort of swim. It's most likely a matter of smell or touch, or both.

A big river roaring along can be an intimidating sight, but again I think we are more frightened by such speed than many fish species. Of course, fish will look for some sort of respite from the storm and if we find these places, almost certainly fish will be there.

The key is to find a swim where you can get some upstream shelter from a fallen bush, trailing tree, rock outcrop or whatever. With such a feature behind you, you can fish downstream and across the river for a surprising distance and often hold bottom a good way out with not too much lead. You'll still have some sensitivity in the line if you decide to touch leger, or some play in a quivertip if this is your preference. It may take some time to build up a swim but stick at it because the fish are almost certainly there or thereabouts and can be goaded into feeding despite the height and force of the river.

Never underestimate the intelligence of this particular species!

Big chub look for a combination of factors in a stretch of river. Here they have everything – tree cover, a push of water and a slack area to repair to in floods.

perfectly adequate. For bite indication, use either a quivertip highlighted by an isotope or a torch, or a butt indicator. Bites will be so infrequent that touch legering is likely to prove wearisome.

Alternatively, try tracking chub on the faster, more characterful stretches of the river, looking for the spots where you're most likely to find them at home. The places to look for are overhanging trees, tree roots, obvious snags, drop-offs, sudden deep holes under trees especially and so on. Attack these fish with large, juicy, instantly acceptable baits. The key here is to drop the bait right on top of a fish: lowering it down its chimney, so to speak. Bites often materialize within seconds, so it's an exciting approach.

Yet even these audacious chub can be difficult and you can increase your chances by touring the, say, ten or twelve swims that you

Wading out to a slightly deeper hole where chub abound often pays dividends.

intend to fish and putting a tasty sample of the baits in before you offer a hooked one. Luncheon meat is excellent, so is sausage, a chopped worm or bread – or try a piece of cheese. If the bait is big, smelly and visible it should get big chub drooling.

But let's imagine the fish you're after are unusually difficult, and wise to all your tricks. Why not try for them with delicate roach-type tackle, baiting with a couple of maggots on a size 16 hook and perhaps trotting these past a well-known lie? Feed the swim for fifteen or twenty minutes before the first cast, because chub really appreciate free food and this boosts their confidence enormously. Make one cast and if the float doesn't slide under, leave the swim for a while and come back and try again later. Don't persist or the fish will grow even more

suspicious – it's in their nature. Although you should avoid fishing too light – you don't want to lose a fish – it's amazing how big a chub you can keep away from snags by constant pressure on even a roach rod and 2lb line. Just refuse to give it any slack or let it have its head.

The successful chub angler ponders long and hard about his fish and what it's thinking. I once said, with total conviction, that if I could see a chub then I could catch it. Nowadays I shudder to count the number of times I have regretted that idiotic statement. There are some chub that are simply uncatchable in certain water conditions. Or almost – we mustn't lose hope. Indeed it doesn't do to lose confidence about any species, because then you stop thinking clearly about solutions to the knotty problems the fish confronts you with. Just remember: keep calm, keep thinking and you'll keep catching.

Back-end Barbel

In late February and early March the river wakes up at last after the seemingly endless winter. Now the days are longer, with more light and steadily rising temperatures. The snowdrops are wilting, the daffodils are on their way – and the barbel are responding. As the spawning season approaches, it's a time of big fish, of possible monsters. Thickening out now, the fish are developing great shoulders and deep, solid bellies.

Light is very important to barbel, especially in the winter, and you will find that sometimes it sparks them into life. However, on other occasions, when the water is particularly clear and cold, they probably prefer darkness.

There are always perfect days at this time of the year, shining times that help you through the closed season to come, memories of the river that you can store away and replay at will. Let's imagine such a day. You arrive at the bankside at 9 am and it's mild, with hints of sunshine over a river that has dropped from a moderate flood ten days earlier and is now running nicely within its banks and showing a visibility of about 12in. Water temperature is in the very low fifties Fahrenheit.

You start on a glide 100 yards beneath the rapids that you know barbel use for spawning. You're not sure if barbel are there at present – perhaps the water is just too shallow and quick – but the way to find out is to trot. Maggots might do the job but the dace have come back with the warmer

A massive winter fish – notice those broad shoulders. It was taken in a deep swim close to the bank under alders – always a favourite with barbel, especially when, as here, there is some current keeping the bottom clean.

weather and the minnows look as though they would eat a gallon each and come back for more. A lobworm will do the trick here: barbel will respond immediately to it. In water of this colour they can see a lob even when it is 12–24in away and will make a snap decision. It's a bait that will really lever a barbel off the bottom and provoke it into a lunge. The float simply flies under, so that in many cases no strike is needed.

The glide is long, at least 100 yards, so is it best to attack it at the top, in the middle or towards the end, where it begins to deepen a little and steady? There are other promising spots to try during the day, so the best thing is to concentrate on the lower half of the run. You could be missing out on fish, but reason says the slightly deeper, steadier water at this time of year will be productive – if barbel are there in the first place, that is. The depth varies between 5ft and 6ft – perfect for trotting and, as there is no wind, line control is satisfyingly simple.

There's need to bait up with anything, so

A good winter barbel – this one weighed nearly 8lb, whereas in the summer it might not have even scraped seven.

you just work the float hard, trying all lines close to the bank and out into mid-river, feeding the float round the overhanging branch, enticing it into the slack, stopping it on the crease – anything to provoke a take. Two chub and one 5lb barbel later and you decide it's time to move on, half a mile down-river to the boulders, a sure-fire spot for a fish or two.

Stones of all shapes and sizes attract barbel and here some large pieces of masonry have been pushed into the river to shore up the bank as protection against floods. Some have rolled out into mid-river and they dot the bottom here and there as if there has been an underwater explosion. There are nearly always barbel in the vicinity and one actually tops as you approach.

Your heart sings and your fingers shake a little as you tie on the hook and the new terminal tackle. No float this time: here it's best to slow the bait right down on a straight lead that you can lift and move downstream every couple of minutes, slowly searching a patch of water. With the rod held high and the line wrapped round the left index finger, you can both see and feel bites – in short, they're unmissable. The 12ft float rod does the job nicely, and there's no need at all for a quivertip. The bait is large, smelly and instantly attractive – the lobworms will continue doing their job effectively, but so would luncheon meat or sausage or even a piece of cheese paste – a winter bait that is sadly overlooked at present and definitely due for a revival.

There's nothing for a while but there's one spot at the tail of the boulders where alders have started to grow up again and their branches meet the water that you really like the look of. And so do the barbel. The 10lb 6oz fish that you land after an amazing struggle is your best barbel of the winter.

By now, it's late afternoon and time to move another mile downstream towards the deep, dark pool under the willows that you've

A lovely double-figure fish taken after dark in a big deep hole where there was no current at all to help the angler. Night fishing was almost certainly the only worthwhile tactic here.

always fancied. You stopped off there in the morning and put out two cans of sweetcorn and now that whisper of hope inside you is urging you on. There are more barbel to be caught by the boulders you know, but this could be the day of legends.

By five o'clock, you're tucked well into the bank, two quivertip rods made up, both with swimfeeders carrying corn. The pool beneath you is deep, with a reasonable flow, and you want to get bait down there, close to the hook, where it matters. The place is rarely fished, so straightforward tackle like this should arouse no fears at all. Both quivertips are fitted up with isotopes – normally you'd touch leger but this evening you want to use two rods to increase your chances. The pool's a big one and you don't know the hot-spots, so two baits will obviously improve your chances.

Some 2lb of corn has already gone into the swim and each cast introduces more. So, even if there are chub about, you're still confident that the barbel will have found some of the magic yellow seeds.

The noises of the night take over and the river seems to move more quietly – somehow you've always registered this, but never really thought about it.

It's nearly dark: a fish crashes noisily downstream – probably a pike out hunting dace or roach. A bat twings your line and makes one of the isotopes dance. Your mind is going back over the season, the successes, the failures, the challenges met and surmounted. You've drifted back to autumn, stalking some carp, or to the springtime, when you found that large bream, dead after spawning, sadly awash in the shallows. It's then, at about 6.45pm, that your rod slams round and you hit a barn door!

Could this be your dream fish at last, hooked, fleeing down the dark river? The whining clutch, the juddering rod, the heartbeat in your head all tell you why you are a barbel fan.

Choosing a Swimfeeder

Swimfeeders are excellent for getting bait down through the water to the precise area on the bottom where the fish are. You can use a bait-dropper, especially for close-in work, but if you're fishing further out a swimfeeder is hard to beat.

Most anglers regard the block-end feeder as the perfect tool for use in flowing water, and in general they're right. You can use a feeder-link for light tasks and the oval-shaped block-end feeder for heavier work in our bigger rivers. Or try the mini-feeder for block-end work in very cold conditions if you think the fish are not feeding hard. A bonus is that all these feeders will also work well in stillwaters, with maggots and other particle baits .

An open-ended feeder allows you to pack bait inside and then plug the ends with groundbait. This approach works well on both rivers and stillwaters.

In my view the cage feeder is a wonderful device because it releases the bait quite quickly and is hardly effected by the fastest of currents. The ideal combination of benefits.

A great advantage of open cage feeders is that you can stuff them with inanimate objects like sweetcorn which would have a lot of trouble wriggling their way out of an enclosed block-end feeder! Of course, you can also use corn in a block-end feeder with the top taken right off. This works very well for me, especially in the biggest rivers when the flow is heavy.

Choose your feeder very carefully. Make sure that it carries the right amount of the sort of bait that you want to use. Also, check that it has enough weight to hold bottom in the sort of conditions that you'll be facing. Finally, ensure that it is heavy enough to cover the required casting distance without shedding its load of bait on the way.

It is tempting to get to the waterside and be in such a rush that you put the first feeder on the line that comes to hand. Don't. Take a little time to work out as precisely as you can what the conditions require. However effective the feeder in the circumstances for which it was designed, it must be capable of getting the bait to the fish where you're fishing. So, if your first choice of feeder is not working, change it rather than minimize your chances for the rest of the session.

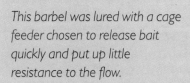

This barbel was lured with a cage feeder chosen to release bait quickly and put up little resistance to the flow.

Canals in Winter

Winter canal fishing can be completely frustrating: I know this fact from years of flogging waters throughout my youth. Still, provided the water isn't cloaked in several inches of ice, there's always a chance of success if you understand how cautiously fish behave at this time of year. The milder the weather the more mobile they will be, and the more they're on the move the more they'll need to feed. But when temperatures begin to fall dramatically you have to think hard.

All the features that were significant in the summer are worth a look: rushes and reeds, long-moored boats, landing-stages and so on, but very often in winter you need to investigate everything, however small, that might attract fish. For example, in plummeting temperatures canal roach will pack tightly against any debris that gives them just that little extra feeling of security: fallen masonry perhaps, a sunken branch – not necessarily a large one – or even a super-market trolley. Anything that breaks up the long, featureless waterway will attract fish.

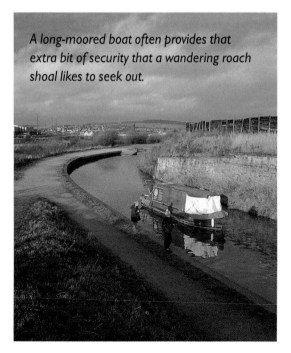

A long-moored boat often provides that extra bit of security that a wandering roach shoal likes to seek out.

There are times in the winter when the odds are so stacked against the angler that it's hopeless to fish before late afternoon. Roach, in particular, will be out and about at that time – if they venture out at all! In summer roach like the last hour or so of daylight, but in winter it becomes critical to feed then, for the dying light offers more security. A water that has been dead all day can come alive with feeding roach when it's almost too dark to see the float under the rod tip.

The most successful canal angler I ever knew refused to bait a swim until he'd found fish. He would move constantly, presenting his bait all round a swim for a few minutes

until travelling on to the next area that he fancied. He reasoned that loose feed simply filled fish that were hardly hungry anyway. His other point was that a free-falling maggot simply showed up the hooked one for what it was – a subterfuge. If the fish had nothing to compare the hooked maggot with, then it would be more likely to take it.

Even when he stumbled across fish, he would keep this idea firmly in mind, feeding sparingly and then waiting several minutes before casting a bait into the area. Once again his logic was that the fish would have become alerted to food, frustrated and more likely to grab at the first maggot or caster they saw

When canals are hit by cold weather the fishing can prove very difficult. Even so, snow is often not too bad – until it melts and brings the water temperature down a few degrees.

without giving it a second thought.

It's risky to credit fish with reasoning powers like this – far more so to suggest that they think like us. But sometimes this approach works, so it can't be discounted entirely. Fish do learn and they do have thought processes, and the Master Angler constantly tries to get in touch with these. It's the most effective way to better your chances during the cold, hard days of winter.

Winter Stillwaters

When Winter Bites

There are occasional winters like that of 1963 when the weather is so cruel that all waters, still or flowing, freeze over and fishing should simply stop. That dreadful winter, possessed child that I was, I carried on fishing with the help of my father's sledgehammer and several yards of rope, and as a result I often came home crying with pain from the cold. Then one day the rope wrapped itself round my ankle and pulled me in after the hammer. Never again, I vowed.

But that was an exceptional time, and winter is normally no barrier to productive fishing. The thinking angler scrutinizes weather forecasts from November onwards, right to the end of the winter. In this way you will develop a keen sense of what the weather is doing and begin to recognize and predict the swings of temperature and the fronts, warm and cold alike. Specifically, you begin to enjoy foreknowledge of when longer periods of warm, wet westerlies are due and, with luck, you'll be able to arrange your schedules accordingly. For in stillwaters in particular, a mild, wet wind gives you your best chances with every species.

The Master Angler will watch sunsets carefully and look fearfully for clear skies and frosts that are falling by dusk. After a blanket of frost an early start is practically useless: there's no point fishing until late morning at the earliest, and for roach or bream not until late afternoon, even if warmer weather is settling in. Pike and perch are to some extent an exception, but even they are sometimes put off if the night has been very severe. Another problem is that you might well find a skim of ice on the lake if you arrive early, and nothing is more frustrating.

In exceptionally cold weather, always try to give yourself the edge by knowing your stillwater, whether large lake or pit, pool or pond, intimately. For example, water birds often keep areas clear of ice, at least through the first frosts, although they have no chance if the ice is really thick. You'll often find that roach and bream, and inevitably pike, are attracted to these areas. The relative warmth attracts a lot of activity, stirring up the bottom, and the feeding is very enthusiastic.

Many lakes and pits are fed by relatively warm springs, which tend to keep specific parts of the water ice-free longer than the rest. We're not talking about a difference in

Left: On winter nights like this you can be sure that there's going to be a frost. No wind and clear skies will mean temperatures tumbling fast – bad news for the next morning's angling.

Right: It really does pay to watch an accurate weather forecast at least once a day. It's not just what's going to happen to the weather next morning or over night that's important – you also need to pick up the long-term trends and see when warm weather is likely to develop.

Left: On cold, clear nights like this you can forget an early start, apart, perhaps, for pike and perch early in the morning if the weather isn't actually freezing.

Below: Waterfowl often keep areas of lake clear of ice with their comings and goings. The fish know this and move to them accordingly.

temperature of a degree or two: springs can be warm enough to have a distinct impact on parts of many stillwaters. Make a note of where these spots are, for roach and bream always congregate there during cold weather. Again, pike are bound to follow.

A bridge across a stillwater deters ice for a while, and the fish know it. My own lake has a bridge on its north-western side and I've

seen fish beneath it so many times that I know it's more than mere coincidence. Sadly, the cormorants have wised up to this as well, and in winter I walk that way as often as possible, shooing them out of the trees.

In fact, the predators of the bankside give many clues to the behaviour of fish. Herons, for example, are the most practised, calculating hunters, and where you see them

A frozen lake is a depressing sight, but there might still be certain areas kept free of ice by warmer springs hitting the surface — especially in shallow water. Also look for areas under trees or round reedbeds where frost might not have struck sharply.

wade in cold weather, to stand still against the frosty reeds, you can be sure that fish move at some time during the day. It may only be shallow, but if fish are there, try to work out why.

Tree-lined areas of any lake or pit are also a good bet when bitterly cold weather strikes, but you must decide for yourself whether it's worth putting up with both the cold and sport that is almost certain to be slow. But there are compensations: for example, carp never look better than they do in winter. With their colours seeming to deepen and their bodies filling out until their muscles are rock hard, they are quite magnificent. As for pike, their spots begin to glow and they're like big, barrel-chested leopards when you catch them – far removed from the slimy, often slender fish of summer. Catch a big female pike on a bitter January day and you will first gasp and then laugh at the weather, however cold.

Winter Carp

Tackling a large, clear pit with a small head of big carp in winter demands great tenacity, and even a skilful angler with plenty of knowledge of the water will find it gruelling. It's wiser to concentrate on small, better-stocked waters where you can be fairly sure that your bait is close to a carp. On waters like this you are at least learning something while you're watching fish and thinking about why you're not getting bites or, just as usefully, why you've just landed a fish.

When you're fishing a huge water and getting no response you don't really know if your approach is right or wrong – it may just be that there are no fish in your particular area. You need a database of knowledge – something that smaller, more intimate waters yield up more readily.

One of the most obvious clues in a smaller water is the presence of a sizeable snag. In

Left: A superb winter carp displaying dramatic colours. This fish was taken from the shelter of some over-hanging alder trees – a deep, dark, shaded place of the kind that the carp seem to love.

Above right: You should not underestimate the rewards of winter carping, as this handsome fish demonstrates.

Right: A winter carp almost beaten as the light begins to go.

Time for a quick flash shot before another good fish is returned to the winter lake.

where there's usually more food.

Sunlight is also an important factor, and winter carp love its warmth. It galvanizes them, wakes them out of a stupor and makes them think spring feeding times are on the way. And, of course, it warms shallow water up more quickly than deeper areas – another reason for fish to frequent the shallows.

In winter – and, to a lesser extent, in summer – carp seem to favour being at a particular depth and don't really rise up or move down much deeper. This preferred level may be anything between 4ft and 8ft below the surface, although they will also frequent whatever other depth suits them at the time. Although they will vary this depth, very often they seem reluctant to do so. At such times, if they drift at a particular depth across an area of lake bed that holds food, they might very well take it.

Having witnessed this phenomenon many times when the water has been clear enough, I'm convinced that it points to the approach you should adopt. In short, once you've found the depth at which the carp are hanging you need to find the areas where the bottom meets this level. When you have done this you will probably have located their current favoured feeding depths.

As for the preferred feeding times of winter carp, unfortunately you can never quite be sure. Sometimes they feed at night but very often they do so in the early afternoon, when the sun is at its highest. The trick is to spend as many hours at the water as you can, building up a detailed picture of their feeding habits.

What is clear is that, apart from very rare occasions, the carp will not be feeding with the gusto they showed in summer. Therefore you must bait less, bait accurately and offer a food that they really want. Most successful winter carp anglers use baits with strong flavours and put in only a few samples, usually on a PVA stringer.

winter fish are more slow-moving than they are in summer, and like to stay near some sort of obstacle, such as a fallen tree or a died-back bed of lilies. Both of these are favourite winter carp locations, and if the water is clear enough you'll see fish there. Other prime spots are under overhanging willows or alders, around an island or among the supports of a boathouse.

Of course, finding carp in such an area doesn't always mean that you'll catch them, for often they will be semi-comatose, barely moving in and out of the fallen branches or other obstructions. What is encouraging, however, is when you see carp begin to move. Perhaps surprisingly, this often occurs in shallow water. Most winter carp fisherman are entranced by the mystique of deeper water: evidently the word got round that you hunt winter carp in deep water, and it seems to have stuck. In fact, if carp are feeding, then they will be rooting around in shallows,

Pike Location

Winter pike are at times infuriatingly moody and therefore extremely hard to catch. It goes without saying that your bait should, as always, be the best you can muster and should be well presented. However, the main problem when you're after difficult pike is not bait or presentation but simply finding the fish in the first place, especially on large, featureless pits, lakes and reservoirs.

Look out for feeding fish and for prey fish topping and scattering in a panicky fashion. The explosive roar of an predating pike makes the choice of swim even more obvious. But unfortunately pike aren't always as obliging as this. One good tip is to have a lure rod ready for use, even if you are putting most of your faith in livebaits or deadbaits. A lure allows you to work big areas of water and gain an idea of whether or not pike are about. The odd tug or two might confirm their presence, even if you don't land the fish. Or

sometimes a pike will follow your lure in, so always wear Polaroids to help you see as soon as possible both the device and what is pursuing it.

Don't worry if all you're catching on the lure is very small pike – a big female may well be hanging around, especially in late winter when spawning time is drawing near. Once you have located a group of pike, you can set about catching them in your preferred way.

Drifting over a wide area in a boat is, as well as being a means of reaching fish that would otherwise be well out of casting range, a wonderful way to locate pike on a large water. The mobility it gives you, and the way that you have to work constantly at it to get results – it's never boring – make drifting a joy of a method.

Trolling, where the rules of the water allow it, is also an excellent way to find groups of pike. Once you've taken a fish, simply lower the anchor and saturate the area

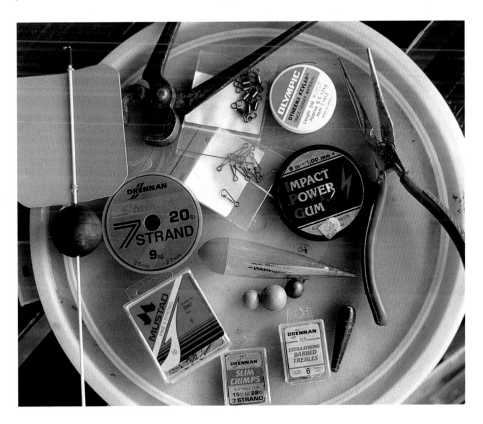

Everything the drift fisherman needs to make up his rig.

Left: Two enormous pike that came from a tiny depression on the north-eastern bank of a pit. These and other fish were holed-up tight and baits had to be placed accurately on top of them or no run would result. It's at times like this that a tethered bait – either legered or float-pater-nostered – really pays off.

Below left: A small and beautifully marked winter pike caught at distance on the drift float.

Below: This lovely fish was taken close in once a shoal had been located.

The Drift Float

The diagram makes it clear how the drift float works: that big sail catches the wind and with ease 'yachts' a bait anything up to 150 or even 200 yards from the bank.

But what are the keys to successful drift-float fishing? First, don't neglect the close-in margin. Try to get your float drifting from right under the rod tip to the farthest limit at which you want to fish. It's tempting to cast the float and bait well out into the main body of water, but by doing so you often miss close-in fish .

Make sure that your rod, reel and line are up to the job, as this method is really punishing. And, when it comes to lifting and mending line at long range, it's best to use a lengthy rod. Take no risks with the line whatsoever: always check it for abrasions and make sure that it's well greased – with the auto-greaser if necessary – to keep it riding on the surface. Always use line of around 15lb b.s. and keep the spool filled right up to the lip. It pays to change the line after every three or four days of fishing as it takes an awful lot of pressure.

A drift float works best in winds of force 3–5. Lighter breezes sometimes shift it too slowly, while gales often whip it right out of the water. Therefore in very light winds, don't use too much weight under the float and in strong gales put on a bigger drift float and heavier leads.

Make sure that the size of your bait suits the capacity of the float because if you have too big or too lively a bait it will pull the float down and the drift will never get under way. Livebaits are particularly effective under a drift float but deadbaits work too, especially if mounted head down or even horizontally.

Don't be in a hurry to get your float as far away from the bank as possible. Every ten yards or so, stop the line from flowing out and this will have the effect of making the float plane backwards and forwards in front of the wind, often covering a channel of some twenty yards in width. This way you can really cover a lot of ground slowly and methodically.

Never let your eyes stray from your float – when it's at some distance it can be difficult to see a bite even when you're concentrating on it. Once the float goes under, strike at once if it is a long way from the shore because by the time you have wound in slack line and made contact the pike could have taken the bait deep down. When you're fishing at very long range the most effective way to set the hooks is to wind in until everything is tight and then walk backwards up the bank, striking as you go. Eventually you will feel the fish's resistance.

Drift float

Stop knot

Bead

Barrel lead/bullets

Bead

with baits. Wait at least half an hour before you write the troll-caught fish off as a fluke. Be careful not to overdo trolling, though: in shallow, fairly clear water in particular, the constant toing and froing of a boat can alarm fish over a wide area. For this reason it's a method to be used sparingly.

Never discount historic hot-spots – those favourite areas that yield up fish year after year. Often these places include drop-offs or gullies, but sometimes there's no clear reason for their enduring popularity with the fish. It's not unusual for fish after fish to be caught from very small, tight areas of a very large stillwater throughout the winter without there being any definite clue as to why they are there. It's evident that pike know better than we do what they want from an area. However, the more you come to understand that particular water the more likely you are to be able to pinpoint these places and extract pike from them.

Possibly the first area to search on any stillwater, large or small, is the banks to the north and east because these receive the prevailing southerly or westerly winds. It's well known that prey species tend to follow the winds and on all waters pike will move to the north and east when they're hungry to find small fish or await their coming. Often the start of a big wind that stirs up the whole water can galvanize comatose pike into feeding – and this can be dramatic after a long period of inactivity.

Spice up your Deadbaits

Deadbaiting is sometimes regarded as the lazy piker's option but this view is far from accurate. To enjoy success with deadbaits you've really got to put your mind to it.

First of all let's look at the variety of deadbaits available, because too many anglers use the same tired options without ringing the changes. Pike learn, like any other fish. You have a wide choice of bait fish: freshwater species such as roach, perch, bream, dace, chub and even small carp are all excellent on their day. Consider too the less common options: eel sections and small rainbow trout – both stunning baits at times. Then there are the sea species – not just the proven ones such as herrings, mackerel, smelts and sardines, but also the exotics that you can find at a really good fishmonger's – scad, big sprats, gurnard, goat-fish, small mullet and sea bass, or indeed anything else on display that looks worth trying.

Having selected your bait, you can enhance its attractions in various ways. For example, 'popped-up' deadbaits are very well worth trying. Simply pack a few with polystyrene or foam to make them rise above the bottom weed and sway around in the current. Food dyes also work wonders, especially on hard-fished waters where the pike have seen most baits. Red and orange seem firm favourites with most innovative pikers. Finally, you can inject deadbaits with flavours – increasing the oil content in this way makes the smell billow around them.

To preserve your deadbaits mark each packet clearly with what is inside and store them in an orderly and accessible fashion in your freezer. There's nothing worse than trying to sort out a jumble of unidentifiable baits at five o'clock on a January morning. A well-organized freezer is a must for every pike angler.

Index